I Took It As A Sign
by
Susan Ashton-Burghley

148 PAGES

E-mail:
dandapress@gmail.com

ISBN-13: 978-1505564808

Many thanks to Sony Entertainment, for permission to use the quote
from *Sisters Of Mercy*, from the album *Songs Of Leonard Cohen*, by
Leonard Cohen.
http://www.leonardcohen.com/ca/node/1186

Cover: Photograph – The Author in a Family Photograph

D & A
PRESS

This Book is dedicated to:

Dawn & Sheila

Reflections of Unconditional Love

I Took It As A Sign

by

Susan Ashton-Burghley

D & A
PRESS

I TOOK IT AS A SIGN

ABOUT ME

This is a story which involves many facets of human life, from love and light, to the darkness of abuse and the embodiment of evil itself. There are parts that are deeply disturbing not only because of the inherent nature of the acts but more importantly because of the devastating effects on consciousness. When abuse happens, our natural aversion from wanting to know 'why me' can keep the emotional devastation alive and influential throughout a lifetime, held in place by the mind's ability to block what we can't bear to remember.

Yet while we can block the details of experiences from our conscious awareness, there can still remain a feeling that something bad has happened for as the saying goes, 'the body knows'; that's the truth. It's like the great recorder, every experience you've had in life is held in the body as memory in the form of a feeling. Feelings that can be explored further if you dare to ask 'why me' because you feel ready to do so, or feelings that spring forth involuntarily when external events trigger them to do so, such as what happened many times with me. But regardless of how you become aware, how do you go about getting past the devastation? The ways are as unique as we are individual, but available to us all. I believe so are the answers, if your will is to know.

This is my own personal story, demanding that I be open and honest in my sharing. No way around that if the truth is to be told and freedom is what you seek, and even if it can be painful in the process, it's what sets you free. While I've inherently known this to be true, twenty-five years in law enforcement, several of those being a police officer, gave me ways to hide from my own internal knowing and pain. In essence, I could hide behind my work persona. It was a protection I could call upon at will. I felt insulated from any unwanted influence of others and the work I chose, in part, reflected this.

Surveillance became my field, covert and top secret in terms of what or who I worked on. No one, including boyfriends, friends and family knew the details of this part of my life, even where I physically went to work everyday.

How did I come to be in this work?

At that time my father worked for a security company expanding operations to the airport. He didn't work there, but they needed personnel so he suggested I apply. My brother was at the airport too in his first posting as a firefighter so almost on a whim, I applied and got the job.

I was posted at gate entrances along with the police who were required back in those first days of airport security, and it was those new police associations that opened the doors to the covert world I describe above. In hindsight, it's a little ironic that it did begin with my father because he was one of those unwanted influences that I wanted to be protected from. He didn't know that because I didn't let it show, but my becoming a police officer at the age of twenty-four made a difference. He somehow didn't feel the freedom to come at me the same way he had before, at least not as often.

In my police work, the 'need to know' component was welcomed and honoured by me. I was after all, very good at keeping secrets, many years of practice doing that. I didn't even think about how this protected environment served me in not realizing the extent of my own vulnerabilities, at least not on a conscious level. My work on high profile cases kept my life interesting yet I felt I was lacking something at the same time. And while it was important to me, and influential in my life, my work did not wholly define who I was.

It certainly did not fill the emptiness I was beginning to feel inside. I had a great job, good friends, and my precious dog Tammy, a friendly yet very protective golden lab retriever who was a constant, always at my side. When I moved from the house I shared with friends, she was like my security blanket. I moved to a townhouse with a yard so at least she had somewhere to play when I wasn't there. I had nothing to complain about right?

It was true, but within me there was a longing, I really had no idea for what. I needed to explore, and thus began my search for something to replace the feeling of isolation that had once felt like my protection.

It was while I was in that townhouse in the eighties that I began to explore what I now see as a spiritual quest, a continuing evolution of understanding myself and those around me. I started with the traditional approach of taking college courses in psychology, but nothing really held my interest.

I wasn't getting to that place where I felt any kind of peace or sense of purpose so, when my friend Sheila asked me to sign up with her for a course on self development with some people she knew, I went willingly. After all, she was my trusted friend, and I had been internally asking for some new direction. You know what they say though, be careful what you ask for because sometimes the getting there may include travelling down roads you wouldn't otherwise choose.

It turned out that the workshop was based on 'new age' thinking, the self-help books had been channelled and the approach was metaphysical instead of psychological, all about sharing from the heart. This was a unique approach for me at the time, and I went willingly but truth be known, I was cringing inside. After all, I was a police officer, and to be sitting around with a group of strangers sharing my feelings, which is what these people were doing, was a little weird for me. In fact, it was way out of my comfort zone.

I think I was outside of their comfort zone as well. No one asked me outright but I sensed a questioning of what I was doing in this circle of 'spiritual' people because the words law enforcement and spirituality were not then, nor to this day, often referred to in the same sentence. After a few times together however, pre-conceived ideas about who I was based upon what I did for a living gave way to openness to understand that I was more than the definition of what my work might present.

A case in point was the concept held by many that my intuitive ability was something that came from my being in police work, when the truth is, it was the other way around. I used my intuition to guide me on a regular basis in my work, from locating a subject lost in surveillance, all the way to disseminating intelligence from a wiretap to an investigator. The timing and sharing of relevant information can be crucial, and sometimes all I had to guide me through to what might be relevant to share at the right time was my intuition. I brought that into my work.

Thanks to my knowing friend Sheila and in spite of my initial resistance, this workshop brought a whole new set of references into my life and marked the beginning of further exploration into the mind, body and spirit connection. I also wanted to know more about recognizing and being aware of the 'energy' behind all that isn't seen nor understood by the intellect; that which is received intuitively.

While my strong analytical mind would keep me looking for traditional sources of learning, my intuitive sense was also telling me, if you want to know the truth, be open to let life bring you the teachers you need, unorthodox or not. I wanted to learn to develop and absolutely trust this inner source of knowledge but where would I find someone who could teach me this?

I was given the answer to this question a few years later, after receiving an invitation through a friend to attend a weekend seminar in Vancouver. All my friend could tell me about the facilitator, Dawn, was that she absolutely trusted and lived by following her inner guidance. He didn't really need to tell me any more.

Dawn, my teacher, mentor and dear friend became an integral part of my life from that year we met in 1986 to her passing in 2008. It was an incredible journey of learning as it relates to self reliance and sourcing from within, more than I could have ever wished for. And it did teach me, undisputedly, that by following my own intuition, doing that which is true for me, will replace any sense of lack with a sense of purpose.

New Years Day 2010

Today is the first day of the year of 2010 and I'm on the sofa recovering and pondering about the lateness of the night before. Was it really after four in the morning when we got home? Oh yes it was, but the fun we had at the New Year's Eve party at my new favourite 'Cheers' style bar and grill called the 'West Beach' was worth it. This quaint little beach front town that's been my home for the past six months has been like that. It's brought new places to explore, and many new people to embrace such as the two friends I'd gone to the party with.

And since I live within walking distance from the West Beach, these two friends, Roy, a former firefighter and his buddy Jamie, walked me home to make sure I got there safely. Since it was so late, and cabs were so scarce, I brought out the extra blankets and pillows to accommodate a few hours of shut eye for these two until they were good to go in the morning. After a few hours of sleep, they went off to begin their new year's day while I happily stayed home to relax.

As I lay on my living room sofa, I looked at my deck of 'Healing with the Fairies' cards that sit on my glass coffee table in front of me. They were a gift, and I leave them on the table for entertainment and the occasional read, which usually happens when friends come to visit. We socialize and when the evening comes to an end, someone inevitably says, 'let's pick a card', so we do. It's all in fun and yet interesting to see how often the card a person picks has meaning specific only to them. So this day while by myself, I pick a card and ask the question, what do I need to do to create all I desire in the coming year?

I want to know it *all*, to do whatever I need to clear the way to receive these desired new experiences in love, friendships, work, finances, the whole big picture. And leave nothing out. The card I 'randomly' pick is, 'Moving Forward Fearlessly' which in part says, 'those gut feelings and dreams you've been having aren't just examples of wishful thinking for change, they represent the germination of new projects and situations that are vehicles for a new mission in life. Don't ignore these repetitive, strong thoughts and feelings and take at least one step today in the direction of making your dreams and desires a reality'.

Considering what had been happening in the past few weeks, this card appeared to be anything but random. I'd been awakened at night with thoughts of events that have happened throughout my life, with no particular order in terms of times of occurrence. Some are recent events intertwined with flashes of memories dating back to my childhood. So what's the connection, and why am I feeling compelled to map out the pieces and connect the dots now?

All I know at this point is what I hear internally, from that inner voice we all possess, which says to write and see the connection, and write like someone else is going to read it.

You need to be honest!

And when do I begin this task?

You know what they say, again, be careful what you ask for, you just might get the answer. So today it is. I begin to write the story, to see the connection between all the feelings, dreams and recurring images that I've been having.

Am I ready to do this?

I do feel a little anxious, but at the same time it feels so right. It's almost like I have no choice in the matter. I have resistance for sure, just as I did when introduced to those new age circles years before. And despite subsequent years of sharing in group settings, I'm still very self conscious when singled out to do so. It's probably a good thing that I don't know what this is all going to look like in its completion. All I know is that I need to forge ahead and see what comes.

Carmel

Several years ago, for my 40th birthday, I was invited to Carmel to join my friend Dawn who, as previously mentioned, was also my spiritual teacher. As we sat having morning coffee in the hotel suite we shared, she began relating a story to me, about a man who was the subject of a prime-time special she'd seen. The man was a CEO, by all accounts happily married and generally successful in his life. The news was that he'd also been arrested for making obscene phone calls. As this man chose to seek counselling, what unfolded was his disclosure of sexual abuse as a child by adults known to him and his family. It involved both male and female abusers.

As I listened to Dawn relate his story to me, I felt a tremor occurring within myself, it was involuntary and disturbing. All I could say to Dawn was, I know this experience! She looked at me with a knowing compassion, the look in her eyes said it all. She knew me well but we'd never spoken of such things, and she wasn't sure why she was to relate this story to me now. All she knew was that I needed to hear it.

This was the first time in my life that my feelings of 'something happened to me' were acknowledged by another. It also brought to mind what happened when I had previously tried to talk with my parents. I was in my thirties, and started by telling them how I remembered being treated by my father in my teens, and questioning why he treated me the way he did. This was met with resistance and denial, and created an alienation between us which only brought about more questions and doubt within me.

I knew then that if I wanted to explore any further understanding of my past I would have to do it without them. Those were the only conscious memories that were triggered within me that day in Carmel. What was more disturbing was that tremor, it seemed to carry a feeling of something more sinister. I couldn't go there yet, just safe to stay with what had occurred in my teenage years.

During my mid teen years, my dad was prone to angry verbal outbursts. Once boys came on the scene, if I was out late, or away for the night at a friend's, my return home could be met by him making crude, sexually debasing slurs implying that I'd been out sleeping around, being promiscuous. So far from the truth because in reality, I was more afraid of boys than comfortable, and tended to stay in the safety of groups. The truth didn't seem to matter though, and all I know is that he could somehow make me feel like the slut he said I was.

It was particularly embarrassing if he did this in front of anyone else.

While I was still in high school, my parents moved us to a small town which was within commuting distance to their work, but too far away from my school so I finished my last two years at a new one. In a new school, and a little self conscious, I was flattered that this popular good looking boy named Garry was paying attention to me.

It was his last year in school, which put him a year ahead of me. On this one night, where he'd offered to give me a ride home from a party, we sat talking in his car, in my parents' driveway. After quite some time, when I was ready to go in, he walked me to the front door. As I opened the door and turned on the hall light, I jumped as my father's voice bellowed from the top of the stairs, "what the hell do you think you're doing?"

He then turned to Garry, "who the hell are you?" He didn't stop his swearing and ranting to hear any answers. His yelling would be loud enough to wake my mom and sister but they wouldn't dare come out to see what was going on. Moments later Garry was gone, and I was left humiliated, shrunken.

After that, when I'd see Garry around, he'd say, with a snicker, "uh, how's your dad?" He wasn't trying to be mean, he just didn't understand. I began to hate my dad for treating me like this, and felt betrayed by my mom that she would allow it, but I understood her fear. She didn't want to make herself the recipient of his verbal assaults. She didn't handle conflict well and he could just as easily turn on her.

And even though I felt betrayed, my own protective walls seemed to give me strength that my mom didn't have, so I later became somewhat of an emotional shield for her, less afraid of him and more willing to fight back. Because they were my parents, I also felt guilty for having these feelings towards them. I did love them and like most abuse situations, it wasn't all bad. I was well fed and cared for, as was my eight year old sister.

Santa always came at Christmas and we were taken on some kind of summer holiday every year. We weren't spoiled by any means but given pretty much what we asked for, within reason of course. My brother, two years older than me, was gone to the navy when I was fifteen so he wasn't around for these times. He never did move back home.

As adults, more so since our parents passed away, contact with my brother and his three grown daughters, and their children, is sporadic to say the least. It makes me sad really, when they were all small I was the auntie they loved to come and stay with and I felt like I had a place in the family. No longer so, except with my sister and brother-in-law who I do have regular contact with.

And I have a precious relationship with their boys, an eight and a twenty year old who I adore. I think they know this, which is why they're able to dupe me into giving them back scratches and shoulder massages on demand. Even though I initially always say, 'no, not now', they persist. Please, 'just five minutes and we'll stop bugging you,' they say as they plunk themselves down in front of me, oblivious to the conversation I'm trying to have with their parents. It's how they manage to get me every time.

Back to my teen years though ... while I understood years later why I had taken on what my father had said about me, all I knew then was that he made me feel dirty when it came to boys and sex. When I asked him why he treated me the way he did, his memory became selective, he didn't know what I was talking about. My mom had been a witness to all of it but I think her fear of his temper kept her passive and silent. My father was not my abuser but his attitudes were sexist and in general he objectified women this way.

This time in Carmel was also the first time that my awareness of this darkness went beyond my intellectual knowing as it was safe to be open from my heart. It was just the beginning of piecing myself back together, and little did I know, it would be like the peeling of an onion, many layers to go through before getting to the core.

Just when I would think I'd have understanding of something, that I'd gotten 'it', I'd be shown by my reactions to life that I had not. Is telling this story another way of getting to that core? Given my past and natural inclination to keep things hidden, it may well be. It will I'm certain, help slice through the layers of that thick skin that I, like many others, have carried throughout a lifetime. All in the name of survival.

Protecting From Within

If abuse happens to you as a child, it can be terrorizing, causing an emotional quivering, a shattering of a once safe and protected world. To survive, you create a place for that child to hide, in the name of protection but your inner world is now split in two. And when it's your survival at stake, denial can be as absolute as truth in keeping the blocks to knowing this in place. You then, as the adult, are left with the task of reconnecting to that child and undoing the influence that's kept you separate from yourself. And is this important?

It certainly was for me. Wherever I was emotionally when the split occurred, was sometimes the emotional level I found myself reacting 'from' as an adult. It wasn't all aspects within myself that were affected, but we've all seen 'childish' reactions or felt 'over reaction' by ourselves or in others to situations that, logically speaking, do not make sense. It comes with a self defensiveness, a charge that can, and usually does, have a basis of formation from unresolved past issues.

And it doesn't matter what took you from knowing your worth, your innocence, or what devastated you; acts of lack of love have many forms that can all lead to this diminished sense of self. What matters now is getting past the split and returning to the wholeness of our being, but how do we make this return to who we authentically are? That process too depends on who we are as individuals.

For me, it's been an orchestration of life, by something much bigger than myself. There was the connecting of seemingly unrelated people and events, by influences seen and unseen, from times past and present which showed me the power of individual consciousness and its influence in what is created in life. They say we create out of what we think and feel about ourselves, even from those aspects within that are denied. This can manifest itself in ways that can bring danger and risk of harm, ways that you might not see coming which was the case with me.

I was dealing with influences that I had no idea were there and denial was only protective to a point. Even before I had a thought to ask for guidance in my actions, a practice I adopted as I grew into adulthood, I know now I was being watched over and protected. After all, how did I know the nature of the duality that existed within me? Consciously, like most people, I wanted all that is good in life, and lived with the best of intentions for myself and others.

But under the surface, there were darker streams of consciousness at play that would say I deserved nothing good, or worse, punishment. So at the same time as wanting the positive, I was attracting what could hurt or potentially do me in because of these negative thoughts that I also felt unable to overcome. And what about the connection between feeling paralysed to change negative thoughts, and keeping parts of my life hidden? There's a saying, 'awareness is everything' when it comes to life transformation so maybe disclosure is a good place to start. After all, nothing can change in secret.

In light of this belief, I'm recounting events and encounters that I have had with different types of sexual offenders, on a personal and a professional level. I hope that, through disclosure, it will lead to freedom from the past and protection for the future. I'm also including these experiences as a way of bringing awareness to what may potentially be in our midst. Not to instil fear, but to create less opportunity for those who have the conscious intention to do harm, particularly to children.

Offenders who abuse children known to them, I'm sad to say, are frighteningly common among us. They take the time to get to know the child, making themselves a part of the child's life in a way that makes them feel safe and loved, like a 'best friend'. This often includes forming relations with families and other friends which can eventually lead to easy access because of the high level of trust that is developed. It's all a part of the grooming process which is a necessary component when luring a child.

It facilitates opportunities for abusers who, once they begin, will assault a child on a repeated and ongoing basis, and even if that child grows and becomes physically strong enough to resist, emotionally they'll be unable to move. It's this emotional manipulation and control, the effects of which can be crippling and long term, that helps to ensure non-disclosure by the victim of these acts that are being performed against them.

There too are predators who are opportunists, and although rarer in our society, they are also adept at victimizing children in ways that are despicable, heart wrenching and cruel. They are the ones that abduct, sexually assault and sometimes murder children not known to them, like child killer Clifford Olson. No time to groom or emotionally paralyse so they resort to drugs or physical force to incapacitate.

It is evil beyond imagination and I have, through my work, looked into the face of this one who epitomized this description. As to reasons why I encountered him in my life at the time I did, would have been anyone's guess. I was, after all, in policing.

It was only years later, looking through the eyes of an astrologer, that I had to consider our crossing paths was perhaps more than incidental to my work. I'll return to the chart later, but first, my experience with the personification of this darkness.

Predatory Behavior

Although his types of crimes against children were a rarer occurrence than those committed by offenders known to their victims, Olson's day to day activities made him 'appear' more normal than you might think. He would depart his house in the morning, dressed in a suit, carrying a briefcase like he was going to work, leaving a wife and a new baby at home. These routine activities are what easily influence our expectations of those like him who may be among us, obscuring our ability to see the potential deviance. I have seen first hand how true this can be.

It was in the summer of 1981, and even though it was not known who was committing such unthinkable crimes, there was no doubt a serial killer out there and the fear in the community was palpable. Children were disappearing, seemingly at random and often. Six children had disappeared in a period of six months, and there would turn out to be more. As part of a surveillance team, I was assigned to follow Olson, a person of interest in these missing and murdered children cases that had been happening in suburban areas around Vancouver.

Although there was great public awareness and pressure on the police to find who was responsible for these horrendous acts, an abundant lack of evidence deemed him not to be more than a 'possible suspect'. At least not until this particular week in August, where his witnessed approach toward a child began to mark the end of his rampage.

The morning started when Olson, now under surveillance, was followed from home to a car rental business where he stayed for a few minutes. He then took a short drive to a second car rental agency, where he was somehow lost to surveillance.

When this happens, losing sight of a target, it can make for some tense moments. In this case, given who we were following and why, that feeling was only intensified. To our relief his absence from view was short lived, we didn't have to wait long before finding him again.

As my partner and I were still in the area of the first rental agency that Olson visited, I decided to stay on the street with an eye toward the business, the last place we'd seen him. I was close to a busy intersection where I would in no way, I thought, draw any particular attention to myself. As I was walking toward the area of the business, from about a half a block away, I noticed a vehicle coming in my direction.

It was Olson behind the wheel, now driving a completely different vehicle than the one we'd previously seen him in. This explained the visit to the two rental agencies. The first one was to arrange for a new vehicle, the second was to drop off the car he'd had for the past two weeks. He then took a cab, missed by surveillance, to return to pick up this new rental vehicle which I now, as luck would have it, spotted him in. Just before he got to my point on the street, though, instead of driving right by, he turned into the driveway of a business just ahead of me, adjacent to the street I was walking south on.

He got out of his car, opened the trunk, feigning to look for something as all the while he was looking at me. It was a bright sunny morning so there was no way to block his view or cover myself with an umbrella or hood from a coat. All I could do was treat him like he was invisible to me and walk on by in this first close encounter. I focused on getting the licence plate of the vehicle he was now in, and communicating that to my team. He got back in his car and left the area.

As I had now been seen by Olson and could find myself on the street with him again, I made a slight alteration in my appearance by changing my hair style and outer clothing. He was unlike any other criminal I'd worked on before. He was an opportunist, and if you were a twenty-something or younger, you almost had to be invisible in order not to get his attention.

Later this same morning I was shown this in no uncertain terms. We had followed Olson to different parts of town, ending up in the area of my own doctor's office which I was now in fact, standing in front of. I'd been dropped off to cover Olson on foot as he was out walking, and he was now about a block away, on the other side of the street. Although he was walking in my direction, at the same time he was also talking with an elderly woman he appeared to have randomly met.

Not socially self conscious, he appeared to have no fear of talking to anyone, if it served him to do so. In this regard, any time Olson made contact with a person, they would be approached after his departure by plain clothes officers to determine the nature of that contact, a practice which would prove to be invaluable. And although he appeared to be involved in conversation with this woman on the street, he was, at the same time, constantly looking around.

At one point I felt that he focused upon me, still from across the road. He was too far away for me to see what he was actually looking at, so my 'gut' feeling is all I had to go on. I didn't think about it at the time but this was how my intuitive sense also guided me, reliably I might add, in what to do next in responding to an anticipated action. Not all things can be anticipated though, as I was abruptly shown a couple of minutes later.

As he arrived at the corner and stopped, the woman continued walking, indicating to me that he may be crossing to my side of the street, by himself. He did just that, and was now about a half a block away. I felt that he was coming to check me out. In surveillance, you never want to make eye contact with the person you're working on so you try to keep your distance without losing control of them. Still in front of the doctor's office, I told my team I was going inside to get cover for myself. Someone else would need to take over and watch from the outside.

Inside my doctor's office, the receptionist looked up, surprised to see me. She seemed to know I didn't have an appointment and was puzzled as to why I was there. I made up a story that I was waiting for my brother, that we had chosen this place to meet. As I went to sit down, I heard through my radio earpiece from my team, 'heads up, he's coming in'. I have to admit it was one of those 'holy shit' moments.

It wasn't fear for myself that I felt, but more a concern about my exposure to him. Besides, in the middle of a surveillance, the last thing you're thinking about is how you might be feeling, you're too busy thinking about what you have to do in terms of your job. Whenever I felt fear, I just pushed it down. I was a master at that, keeping unwanted feelings at bay, and it worked well in times like this. A minute later, Olson walked into the waiting room and sat down across from me. I avoided looking at him but felt his eyes upon me.

At this point I went up to the receptionist, started some conversation again about hoping my brother wouldn't be much longer. I didn't want Olson to think that I might be alone, or to appear vulnerable or approachable in any way. He then departed the office. As this was the second time in the same morning that I'd been in a close encounter with Olson, several questions had to be asked. One of those questions for me was, did he connect that I was the same woman he had seen earlier in the morning?

Did he know he was being followed by the police? And more importantly, would he now still approach or attempt to pick up any children? We didn't have to wait long before we received an answer to that question. When he left the area of my doctors office, he drove in his vehicle for only a few minutes before he stopped to speak to a young girl who we'd find out later was only twelve. As he was speaking to her from inside his vehicle, and although she was always protected by the police that were around her, there was relief within me when he drove away, alone.

He only spoke with her for a few moments. Although he was a suspect in the murders of the other children, there was little evidence connecting him to the crimes. What had been determined, however, was that whoever had been abducting these victims had sometimes been known to tell them a story about owning a construction company, and would offer them work, cleaning windows. This was known but never witnessed until now.

As he departed the area, the girl was approached by plain clothes officers who identified themselves and escorted her home. She was asked about their conversation, and what he had said to her. He'd given her the story of being in construction and had offered her a job. This was what was needed, this was what we'd been hoping for. Coverage would be twenty four hours a day; wherever he would travel, we would go. This blanket authorization does not come without criteria being met, such as was witnessed in this attempt to lure the child.

I often wonder what would have happened had we missed this brief but important encounter with the girl. Olson spent the next days, over a weekend, with his wife and child. He'd taken them to a lake, which of course, being summer, was filled with children swimming. People would have been horrified to know who was in their midst, but there was no risk to the public as he was also completely surrounded by plain clothes police officers.

Besides, as he was playing the role of father and husband which meant putting his deviant behaviour on hold for a while with his family, the darkness of this man did not show itself, at least when in public. A couple of days after the weekend, it was a different story as he made a totally unexpected trip out of the city. Well, it was for the most part 'unexpected' and I say this because I had, that morning, decided to pack a little overnight kit in my work bag, my toothbrush and some toiletries.

I had no conscious knowledge that I'd be going out of town and staying overnight in a hotel when I left home for work that day. I didn't share with anyone that I had packed this extra bag, nor did I contemplate the idea of how or why I'd known to do so. I think because at some unconscious level I worried about what this would say about me, like maybe I was tuned in to him because somehow I understood a part of this evil. I did, but not in the way that I thought at the time.

I had known the darkness but I didn't see it back then as a part of my own memory coming forward from my own bad experiences as a child, that awareness hadn't surfaced yet. Nor did I see it as the gift that I see it as today, that 'knowledge without reason' that's sometimes available to us. I just felt uncomfortable.

Olson departed home early in the morning and travelled by ferry to Vancouver Island. It was the middle of summer so the boat was packed, with many people travelling as foot passengers, young people who might be inclined to accept a ride if it was offered to them. This was a main concern with Olson so he was followed closely on foot wherever he went on the ferry. My partner Bill and I had an eye on him as he stood outside on the top deck which of course was busy with people. We sat like a couple on the floor of the deck, our backs against the outside wall of the inside cabin.

At one point Olson was standing in view just several feet away, looking out over the rail to the water. He then began talking with a girl who after a few moments, and to our relief, walked away. Next, and much to our surprise, he came and sat down beside us on the deck, a couple of feet away, to my right.

Bill was to my left, so with sunglasses on and my hood up because of the blowing wind off the water, I looked at Bill and said, 'holy shit', another close encounter.

Although it had been several days since he'd seen me, because I'd been out of sight being a driver on the team, it was the third time in over a week that he'd been close to me. Despite this, I know he didn't make us as police because he wouldn't have hesitated to confront us, but it did make me wonder what he actually saw when he looked out through those evil eyes. A few minutes later he walked on, and there were no other notable encounters while we were out on the water.

Once off the ferry, he drove to the city of Victoria where he entered an apartment building. We found out later it was a senior's complex where he had apparently committed another theft. After that, he drove to a part of the Island highway that was popular for hitch hikers. Two girls who appeared to be in their early twenties were there, hitchhiking together. He pulled over, they got in his car and began to drive north on the highway. They stopped a couple of times along the way, once to purchase alcohol, and the other to get out at a rest stop.

A short while later, the driving resumed which was routine at first, but out of the blue, became totally erratic. He was driving at an excessive speed, becoming an endangerment not only to himself and the girls but to the public at large. The decision was made to prepare to take him down when as fast as his driving had become erratic, it just as quickly normalized, and he began to drive the speed limit.

The decision still stood to arrest him at the first opportunity. He then abruptly turned off the highway onto a dirt logging road, stopping his car only minutes after leaving the main road. Immediately, numerous police officers were into the bush on foot, and as they neared his vehicle, he was heard yelling at one of the females.

Meanwhile, back on the highway, roadblocks were being set up to intercept him in both directions should he decide to drive back out. Moments later, he did just that and was subsequently stopped for what he believed was only a traffic offence. He had also apparently promised these girls a ride with him back to Vancouver the next day, and we all know what the outcome of that could've been.

I wasn't part of the debriefing with these girls, but I understand during that initial stop they were angry with the cops because their promised ride for the following day had been ruined. I'm sure they learned rather quickly just how lucky they'd been this day as Clifford Olson's arrest was all over the news the same night. As it would turn out, this would also be his last day of freedom.

He was an atypical serial killer in that he targeted both boys and girls who were also of various ages. Between November 1980 and July 1981 eleven children lost their lives. And although my role as a police officer in this case was minimal, and the duration was short, it was for me, one of the most memorable cases I've ever been a part of because his victims were innocent and vulnerable children. I only wish such a turn of events could've occurred months before. This outcome, where two and probably more lives were saved, could not have been predicted any more than the tragic events that happened before this man was caught could have been.

I say this because, even though this was the most important work for me in terms of contributing to Olson's arrest, I don't want to minimize the horror that happened to the children who lost their lives at the hands of this monster before he was captured. And I don't want to dishonour the families of those lost children by not making it clear that the only thing there was to feel good about was in relation to the prevention of more tragic and senseless deaths.

I tell my experience of working this case also because of how it intertwines with my own experiences as a child. I could have met with a similar fate as these children. I have in fact had the thought that because of the age difference between myself and Olson. He actually could have been the man in the car.

Man In The Car

We moved several times throughout my early childhood as my parents worked to build a better life for us. As finances grew, what was affordable changed, so this often enabled a move to a new place and different location, although never far from where we'd previously been. And although the neighborhoods were in close proximity, the moves involved a change of schools, several times.

I think we first lived with and shared space with immigrant friends when I was three to later renting apartments above and behind stores until I was about age six. I remember living in two of those kind of places, before moving into an actual house with a yard. I was six when I first met my friend Darlene who I'm still friends with today. That was also my age when I had my first encounter with a predator-type stranger as I was walking home from Dar's house, only a short block away. As I was going up the lane that our apartment backed on to, a man came up and told me that he'd lost something at the school across the street. He asked if I would come with him to look for what he had lost. I said no, I had to be home.

He said he would pay me a quarter if I helped him, but I still said no. At that point, I had a greater fear of what might happen if I was late getting home than I had of strangers, at least as I recall. I walked home safely and said nothing about it, I thought I might get in trouble somehow. I never forgot it, and I think that might have been my first conscious decision to stay silent, but it wouldn't be the last.

The next time happened when I was about to turn eight, having just finished grade two. I remember this because location determined the school I went to, and I was already at my second elementary school. I use these factors in putting together times and places since we had moved to new neighborhoods so often, but this was the first one we lived in where we had a house with a yard.

This neighborhood also had many families with kids my age and because we played out on the street any chance we could get, many people were familiar. If we weren't in our own backyard, we might be down the street or a block or two away in the backyard of one of our friends. We'd play games like 'kick the can' and 'hide and seek' until we got the calls to come home, and it was common to go back and forth by ourselves. It was a different era back in the sixties. There was little thought of risk associated to children being out on their own, not in my little world anyway, and I know it was the same for my parents.

In light of this, to be asked to go to the store by myself to pick something up for my mom would come without a second thought. It was not an unusual request, I'd often go to the little corner grocery, ever so popular in neighborhoods around Vancouver, to maybe pick up a quart of milk or a loaf of bread. Now, on this day when I was asked, it was after dinner and I was with my friend Linda who had come over to play. We didn't mind going, as we probably held some hope of receiving a treat for running this errand. The store was about two blocks away.

As we neared the corner at the end of our street, a car pulled over beside us. The man in the car asked us where we were going. Of course we told the truth and said, 'to the store'. He asked, 'do you want a ride' and although it was only another block away, it was a long uphill block from this seven-year-old perspective so we just said, 'okay' and got in the car. I was sitting in the middle and my friend was beside the door. When we got to the corner and should have gone straight ahead, the man turned right and then took a left into a lane way.

He stopped behind a house about mid block down the alley. I asked what we were doing here. He told us that his wife worked in the house and he was just waiting for her to finish, then we would continue to the store. I don't know how much time passed, it might have been a minute or five. I don't remember looking at the man, I just remember sitting there right next to him, feeling squished between him and my friend. The next thing I knew, he took my hand and guided it towards him. He then wrapped my hand around his penis, held in place by his putting his own hand on top of mine.

It seemed to be a matter of seconds before this white stuff was squirting out in front of us. We didn't know what was happening, just that it was yucky. Linda was upset too because she had on a new purple coat and he was getting this stuff on it. It's funny what the mind chooses to remember. I don't think she saw that he was exposing himself. I also don't remember going to the store. We must have because we went home and pretended everything was normal. I never said a word to my parents about what happened, I was too afraid of getting in trouble. I felt like I'd done something wrong, that it was my fault that this bad thing had happened. How did I even associate this as a bad thing?

It was years later that something else hit me. When that man placed my hand on his penis, even though I didn't know then what it was called, I had an almost simultaneous awareness that my hand had been on something like that before. With this thought, I felt my little fingers spring open and I began to push toward my friend to get out of that car. I don't know how we did it. All I know is, for some reason, he chose to let us go.

As my life went on I thought less and less about this encounter, and I downplayed the emotional impact by pretty well denying there was any. I told myself that because I remembered the event, and I wasn't actually harmed physically, that I could just forget about it. I had a question though that did start to haunt me. How did I know by the age of seven about these sexual things, these private parts? I'd had some memory flashes, pictures that would come to me but I just pushed them back. They were from a time when I was between the ages of three and five, for sure a time which was prior to my going to school.

My brother, being two years older would've started school and perhaps for that reason, he isn't a part of this experience or these dark memories. I don't even know to this day whether I repeated the story of the man in the car to any of my family. I don't think I did, except possibly to my sister in these later years. I told certain friends for sure, and it's surprising how many people have some similar experiences, not in being picked up and let go by a man in a car, but in having experiences that threatened, or have potentially threatened their innocence and safety as children.

Pre-School

My parents immigrated to Vancouver, Canada from England where they, my brother and I were born. I remember nothing about the trip across the ocean, nor the train ride across the country when going from east to west, but I do remember that the little place we lived when we landed had mice that came out at night when it got dark. My mom would wait until we were sleeping before she would turn the lights out because we were frightened. She was probably scared too.

Only in their twenties, my parents came with nothing except a desire to make a new life for us and themselves, our arrival in Vancouver happening shortly after my third birthday. This move to Canada was a big adjustment, particularly for my mom who hadn't wanted to leave her own family. And we had no relatives here, except for a distant cousin and aunt who were from my father's side. I don't think there was any closeness there either because I have no memory of seeing this aunt beyond my early childhood and rare contact with the cousin.

Maybe this is why I recall a sadness with my mom, I'm sure she was overwhelmed with not much energy left for awareness of things beyond what was in front of her. My father too had little to do with our care as young children so there's no remembrance of any kind of close relationship, or sense of being protected. He was, for the most part, a blue collar worker who held the old but then common view that kids were the woman's work, should be seen and not heard, and his primary role was to go out to work and provide.

Even as we grew up, his involvement mostly increased as the disciplinarian, in response to typical kid behavior like fighting between ourselves or not listening to what we were being told. My mom resorted to the 'wait 'til your father gets home' line and if that didn't work, my dad's hand gesture of his belt coming off, with the verbal threat that it would if we didn't smarten up, was enough to get our attention and stop the unruly behavior. We were sufficiently scared so that the actual use of the strap rarely happened.

Given the times and the mode of survival my parents had to have been in when my brother and I were pre-school age, not to have noticed anything beyond the obvious was understandable. And even if their attention hadn't been consumed with the normal day to day challenges of life, because they themselves were not deviant, they couldn't have imagined what they were unknowingly exposing me to.

Since my parents were trying to build a new life, starting with nothing, my mom did need to do the same as my dad in as much as going out to work to help provide for us. I was still at a pre-school age, and some people who lived nearby were trusted with looking after me. They may have been British because lots of their friends in those days were also immigrants from England. Although at this time, this is nothing more than a guess.

It was only a few minutes walk in the morning with my mom to their door. The woman who received me obviously told my mom that I would be taken care of, and maybe I was, at first. There was also a man there, and another little girl, and while I don't recall her name, I do remember her being naked, many times. The man was naked too, it was part of some kind of routine or game that was being played but I don't remember details about that either. All I really do remember is that I started to feel dread in having to go there but powerless to do anything about it.

Maybe that's why I locked myself in our bathroom one morning because I couldn't tell them what was happening and really did not want to go. If that was my way of calling for help, it didn't work. I wasn't ever supposed to lock the door, and I either didn't know how to let myself out or wouldn't. The firemen had to be called to free me, so I got in trouble for that, creating a fuss and making my mom late for work. I was too young to understand or articulate what was happening to me but I somehow felt, even at that age, it was my fault and if my parents found out what I had been doing, they wouldn't want me anymore. If you're bad, better to keep silent and stay out of trouble.

You learn to please no matter what. Behave and be a good girl; that way, they'll still love you. On the other hand, I felt so betrayed. How could my mom willingly put me with these people? I felt abandoned over and over again as I was taken to that door. It was frightening and utterly confusing, too much for a little one to cope with. Although it was years later as an adult, that I was able to identify these feelings, I believe it was the beginning of the disconnect that happened within me.

It was the only way to survive. Outwardly, I became a painfully shy little girl, and in school did everything to avoid drawing attention to myself. I behaved well and dreaded being called upon to do anything that would bring a focus upon me. I really didn't want to be seen, so better to try and disappear. I wanted to be invisible. We moved from that location before I started school and by the time I got to be seven, I had little conscious memory of those pre-school days, until that incident with the man in the car which triggered some recall of the earlier abuse and emotional fallout. It not only showed me that I'd touched a penis before but that I also knew it to be a bad thing and could not tell because that might make me bad too. Who would love me then?

I was seven and already associated sex with negativity. If there was a connection between sexuality and love for me, it would've been a part of the grooming process, that building of emotional trust that enables sexual abuse to occur without an offender fearing discovery because of their ability to emotionally manipulate. Words like, its 'our little secret,' 'you're my special one,' or 'I love you best,' can be powerful, another ploy used in an attempt to ensure that continued abuse can happen with a certain degree of willingness from a child.

If that apparent willingness eventually gets replaced by fear and resistance to further deviant behavior being forced upon you, 'loving' words from an offender can turn to threats to ensure continued non-disclosure. To avoid this, I would comply, giving away what little power I had to resist and say no. After all, I've done what they've asked before, and did it willingly so now it's my fault that they want it again, even if I do not. I was made to feel that I had no rights to want or say anything different.

As a child, you have no understanding or conceptual ability to make a decision in terms of what's right or wrong, you just do what you are told, for the reasons that are given. As a child, I only wanted to do what pleased, it was my survival. And for the abusers, that 'apparent willingness' justified their despicable acts. And from their point of view, I did it before and acted like I was enjoying it, so what's wrong with me now?

Long Run Confusion

This emotional manipulation is what can cause confusion in the long run and if not understood, can manifest as dysfunction in many adult relations, as it did with me. For many years, the thought of having a partner in marriage was a double edged sword. I'd want the companionship and emotional intimacy but because of my inability to say no, I also saw it as being trapped to have sex even if I didn't want to which was like a nightmare to me.

When women friends would 'joke' about their partners' expectations of having sex, like saying, 'oh, it's the weekend, he's gonna want it' or, 'if I want the garage cleaned I guess I'll have to put out', it never felt funny to me. It took me a long time to realize that what was being triggered in me were feelings that came from these pre-school experiences. The option to say 'no' did not exist as that young child and I carried that sense of powerlessness and misplaced ability to respond even as an adult.

It was a learning process, and experience in different relationships, that brought me to terms with understanding the source of my inability to say no to sexual advances. For the most part, I consciously brought what was good and loving to myself. But when denial is in place, what is held at the unconscious level can also manifest, as it did for me, as unwanted and inappropriate sexual or predatory behavior. It represents the more sinister side of what I invariably drew to myself. All I can say is, but for the grace of God …

Drawing The Dark Side

I was walking home from a friend's house on another summer evening, when a man in a car stopped and asked me for directions. I was fourteen, and even though we'd lived in several different locations in the city, it was always the same vicinity so I knew this middle class neighborhood well. I told the man where he needed to go and pointed him in the right direction and started walking away. But instead of driving the way he should have, he began slowly inching his car alongside me as I continued to walk towards home. He tried talking to me through his passenger side window as he drove, but I ignored him, that is until he pulled over and parked. He was getting out just as I passed his car.

Something in me panicked so I started running and so did he. He was now chasing me. In my fear, I ran up to the house of a stranger and banged on the door. When the lady answered moments later, he had just reached the end of the sidewalk leading to her house. I asked, 'can I use your phone?' She must have seen how scared I was and let me in to make the call to my parents. No phoning the police in those days, and the guy just walked on by. Even though 'nothing' really happened this time, I felt terrified.

Was it because of the time with the man in the car when I was seven? Did that emotional imprint now surface as the fear that pushed me to run to that house, like a warning sign for potential danger? I'm sure it did, but what if there's no conscious past to draw on? And what does it mean to be the innocent victim of random behavior? Like being chased by this stranger, or being indecently exposed to by men in public, like at the mall or outside my ground floor apartment window. These things have also happened but why to me?

I had no connection with these people so you'd think it would be easy to reconcile that their bad acts had nothing to do with who I was. I did wonder though, I seemed to have had an inordinate amount of encounters or close calls with men with deviant behavior compared to those around me. Consciously, I saw myself as healthy, physically and emotionally and considered my life to be 'normal'. I've known men who were balanced in their sexuality and appropriate in their behavior, but I've also drawn those who reflected a darker side.

The confusion and negative associations to sex or sexual acts that I'd carried around since childhood were still alive within me but more or less denied. I didn't connect this duality in terms of the influence it would have in my life but it was there. I've had many negative experiences, yet I've remained to a surprising degree quite innocent and open in my response to new people and situations. I'm not suspicious by nature and generally speaking, let myself be guided by my intuition. By definition, it's knowledge without reason and sometimes, when presented with people whose agendas are hidden, its presence can be invaluable. It's a gift which has been progressive, in terms of my own learning to interpret, rely on, and more importantly, listen to. It can also be a warning voice.

Deception

It was in the '90s so I was well into being an adult, happy in my work and generally enjoying my life. I was single, living downtown in a high-rise apartment with an ocean view. This one particular day, I was sitting outside on my balcony enjoying the late afternoon summer sun.

When the phone rang I was ready for it to be one of my friends, maybe wanting to go for a walk along the beach. Surprisingly, it was a man's voice I heard. He asked, 'is this Susan'? I answered and said, yes it was. He asked if I was the blonde that lived in apartment 1402? 'Yes' I said, but 'who is this'?

He told me his name and began to politely explain that he also had a friend that lived in my building, and while he was visiting that friend, he'd seen me getting off the elevator. He knew it might seem a little strange, phoning me like this but he thought I was attractive and wanted to talk to me so he took a chance and called. He gave me his first and last name and told me where he lived. We talked for awhile and he suggested we meet for coffee. He asked, 'could we meet this evening', as it was still early. I thought, well why not? I was a little intrigued, and he was quite charming on the phone. He would drive to my area, and I could walk to the coffee shop which was about a twenty minute walk away.

I'd never done anything like this before but I thought, this might be fun and I love being spontaneous. 'God's flexible angel' is what my friend Dawn used to call me. What harm could be done? I'd meet him for coffee. I did look up his name in the phone book and it was there, with the number he had given me so he was telling the truth, right? He said he knew one of my neighbors so, I'm sure this will be fine is what I told myself. I got ready and an hour later I was meeting him at the coffee shop. He had told me what he'd be wearing so I'd know him, I told him what I'd be wearing too. Of course I didn't need to because he already knew what I looked like, or so I thought at the time.

After finishing our coffee we continued our visit and walked down to the beach. The conversation was easy and I found him to be quite attractive, but the sun was now setting and I felt it was time for me to walk home. He then suggested that he could give me a ride. I did have an immediate reaction, like a knee jerk 'no' within myself but outwardly I just said, 'that's okay, I can walk'.

He began to insist, not forcefully but just enough for me to hush my own inner rumblings and say okay. His car was parked minutes away from where we were sitting so we walked there and I got in the car. I couldn't believe the panic that hit me.

Outwardly, I know my fear didn't show but inwardly I was thinking to myself, what are you doing? You don't even know this person, he could take you and abduct you, no one even knows you're with him or where you are. True and alarming thoughts for sure but not as disturbing to me as my inability to say no to getting into that car. The ride to my place took only a few minutes and before I knew it we were stopped in front of my building.

My relief, although tremendous, was outweighed by my shame for putting myself in this potentially dangerous situation. I quell these feelings by going into a state of denial and minimizing what just happened. I asked myself, what **is** this panic about? I really never think like this, where's this coming from? I'm sure he's not a bad person, I can't be that 'off' about someone can I?

I talk myself into dismissing what I thought at the time were just crazy, paranoid thoughts. I quiet the voice. We sat for a few moments talking, everything seemed normal, everything was okay.

He asked to walk me to the door of my building. Not necessary, I think to myself, but out loud I say 'okay'. As I'm opening the front door, he asks about seeing my view so with my permission, and his promise to stay only a few minutes, he rides up the elevator with me. He steps inside my apartment, checks out the view and moments later starts to leave. On the way out, he stood behind me, wrapped his arms around my shoulders and jokingly said, while facing the mirrored hall closet door, don't we make a nice looking couple? I just smiled in agreement.

A couple of days later he called to see if I wanted to go for dinner. I had mixed feelings but felt compelled to go for some reason. We decided to meet at a restaurant near to where I lived so I could walk the five minutes to meet him. As we were eating and talking our way through dinner he said he had something he wanted to tell me. It was about how he'd come to find me, he hadn't actually been truthful.

First of all, he did not have a friend in my building. I asked, 'how did you know who I was then'? He said he didn't know who I was or what I might look like. He had picked my name randomly out of the phone book. I started to feel sick inside. He said he had just guessed at my hair color and when he got that right he felt more encouraged. He had manipulated the conversation so he would get some further description of me.

As he was speaking, the nausea I was feeling was coming up to my throat. I couldn't get out of there fast enough. But I also felt scared of him at this point so I just listened to him tell his story and pretended it was no big deal. I didn't want him to know just how creeped out and disgusted I felt. I finished my dinner and left to walk home by myself, it was only a block away. I had no further contact with him.

How could I have been so naive and gullible? And even though I came to no physical harm, I did wonder. Did he actually have more sinister intentions that for some reason were aborted? Is that too why my reactions were so strong? Why he decided to tell me the truth of his game I don't know. All I know is that I can be grateful for what he showed me about myself. Disturbing to me as it was, I saw I still felt just like that child who kept the secrets long ago. But it was worse now because, after all, I was an adult and should know better. I never talked about this experience, even to my closest friends.

Shame and self blame can have that effect, overriding any feeling of self love or letting in the love of others. We feel diminished and not worthy of understanding so why open ourselves to further negative judgment. It felt easier to stay quiet about such things, at least that's what my critical self told me then.

And if I didn't put myself in a similar circumstance again, being with a stranger who I'd had some eerie feelings about, then that would help keep me out of harms way right?

Unfortunately, I found out otherwise, for sometimes even the people you think you know can have a hidden and sinister side.

Without Warning

A few years after the above encounter, still in the nineties, I'd moved from downtown to an apartment in a well established residential neighborhood. No beach front but I still had a beautiful panoramic view.

I was also now selling real estate, part of a temporary move away from the law enforcement field which I returned to in

2001. The condo I'd just sold needed some renovations and because my client was also a friend, I assisted her in getting this done before she moved in. She was my mom's age, on her own and a little vulnerable so she preferred that I handle the dealings with the trades guy we'd found.

His name was Mike, and partly because he came with references from someone in the building where my client had just purchased, he was hired. I held the keys to the condo so I'd be there to let him in to do the work.

He'd call when he was finished, and I would come back to lock up, a routine that happened several times. My friend came periodically to see the progress he was making and was more than pleased.

'He's just so nice' she would say. I agreed, he was quick to laugh and make a joke. He was also quite a charmer. He and I were in our thirties, and during the course of these brief exchanges, we'd chat a little too. I obviously knew what he did for a living, but also learned he lived in the city, and had a girlfriend who I believe he said was a live-in partner.

When the work he was hired for was completed, and for reasons I can no longer specifically recall, he was going to be coming by my place to pick something up. It's not unusual in real estate to go to someone's home to pick up items like papers, keys and cheques if it's outside of office hours and you're dealing with someone you know. Or in this case, at least someone you think you know.

He arrived at my apartment, we chatted for a few minutes and then he left. A few moments later he rang my buzzer, he'd forgotten his phone. I hadn't noticed before but now saw it was on my dining room table.

Back up again at my apartment, he came inside the door which placed him in my dining room. It was a small and open plan, so a couple of more steps put him on the area rug that formed a part of my living room. We were standing at my dining table when suddenly he faced me, standing a little to the side.

He then grabbed both of my upper arms, placed one leg behind my leg so I would have no balance and pushed me backward to the ground, flat out on my carpet. It was a matter of seconds. I was shocked, was he joking? It didn't register right away that he wasn't. Half laughing, out of sheer disbelief I said, 'what the hell are you doing'?

He was sort of laughing too but not listening to me. 'Come on' he was saying, 'you know you want this'.

I was struggling but he had my arms pinned down and started trying to kiss and grope me.

He's scaring me now but I don't want to make him angry so I just kept saying, 'please, just let me up'. He then stood, pulled me up but just as quickly pushed me back down on the couch.

He pinned my arms above my head with one hand, and with the other ripped open my pants and shoved his hand down. I tried to wriggle my way out from under him but he was strong, I couldn't move him off me. I don't know what else I said, or why, but before assaulting me further, he stopped. He got up and left.

I was so shaken and again, I told this story to no one. He actually called me the next day, saying something about meeting for coffee, like nothing had happened. I knew that this was his way of 'normalizing' what he did, and maybe trying to see what kind of reaction he would get from me. If I seemed okay, he would get away with what he'd done. I let him think I was fine and I never did see him again.

He was overpowering, and because of my tendency toward self blame and feeling responsible for having him there in the first place, he too got away without any consequence.

At the time, my belief in the 'you must have done something to ask for it' attitude, even if I did say no, was still a part of what immobilized me from saying anything to anyone.

Silence still felt like the only option, the only safe thing for me to do at the time.

Street Angel

What I have wondered about the above incident was why I didn't see it coming?

And you hear this question often when someone is victimized, 'Didn't you see it coming'!? It's almost accusatory sometimes, like somehow you should've been more aware. How are some people able to move around undetected, what makes this possible?

When I recently heard the phrase, 'street angel' and learned of its meaning, I started to have a sense of how this can and does happen.

It came while talking to a friend about my grandfather, in the context of trying to understand the abusive and angry nature of my dad. I'm told my grandfather was liked and known to be the life of the party at the pub but once he got home behind closed doors with my grandma and their children, his actions told a different and darker story.

He was angry and abusive, a side he never showed to the outer world. In listening to my words, my friend nodded and said, ' street angel'. What does that mean? At first I didn't get it. He then explained, you know, when they're out in public, they're on their best behavior but it's only an act, a good act that they use for when they're out, out on the street so to speak.

For some reason, the person in the previous chapter came to mind, would this apply to him? He had assaulted me but was someone who had presented himself as a really nice, hard working, funny, charming guy, who also had a live-in girlfriend. A challenging but necessary facade to keep up especially if you care how you are viewed by the world around you. This act is often mastered by those who have secret lives, or those trying to hide 'behaviors' that would be morally unacceptable at best or at worst, criminal.

It's what sets a 'street angel' apart from those who you do get a 'bad vibe' from, or have a sense that something is just not right. I think those who master the street angel act have one major trait in common, a desire to fit into society and to appear to be what is considered normal. They have a great investment in maintaining that image and keeping whatever else they have that represents that image intact.

To that end, they are master manipulators, adept at keeping their secret sides hidden, unless they have chosen to make you part of it. Like the husband who beats his wife or the predator that molests his own child.

Or, as in my noted, 'street angel' an offender who assaults those known to him and counts on previous association to provide a defense for his behavior, not unlike what happens in many date rape cases. This is why you don't see them as they approach.

And if they are threatened with being exposed for who they 'really' are, they count on the vulnerability of their victims to protect them and keep their dark side hidden. Such as with someone like me who kept silent. And while keeping silent was not always the wisest choice, it felt like the only choice, especially when you're doing so because you think disclosing their acts might say something negative about 'you'.

While writing this story, I've wondered how far beyond this pattern of thinking I was, in relation to myself. I didn't have to wait very long before I would be given a chance to see. Another encounter with a 'street angel' perhaps.

Fast forward from the previous experiences in the 90s, to the spring of 2010, when I was given another chance to see whether I'd keep a 'secret' out of some belief that it might come back to say something negative about me. Even if it's only through my own self judgment.

The Phone Call

I took a two week break from writing, mostly due to the arrival of the 2010 Olympics to the city of Vancouver. While the intensity of this writing parallels the excitement of these games it represents opposite ends of the emotional spectrum. So in order to fully embrace the joyfulness and most collective sense of national Canadian pride I've ever seen, I would put the writing aside. After all, taking in those competitions and imbibing with the many has it's own demands on time and energy but it's been so worth it. I have never heard the words, 'sorry', ' no worries', ' isn't this awesome' and, 'can you believe this weather' repeated so many times in a day.

The masses of people were bigger than we've ever seen on the streets of our city. It's been a fine interlude but, as the end was nearing, I had thoughts of where to go next with this unfolding story. How to get back into the deeper flow after all of this lightness? I even wondered for a moment whether I wanted to continue, it's such a contrast of experience.

Could I delve in again, do I need to?

A phone message I received answered that question, leaving no doubt in my mind, especially given what I've written about so far. It was actually less than a week before the end of the Games. I'd been out with friends watching a do or die hockey game for Canada to win the gold. As history knows, the game was won by Canada so I went home to bed with that 'all is good' feeling that happens when you're an avid Canadian hockey fan. I hadn't been asleep for long when the ringing woke me up. I looked at the clock and it was after midnight.

Who'd be calling at this time?

I let the call go to voice mail but then thought I should check for messages. After all, maybe someone was in distress. I wish I'd waited until the morning to do this, at least I would've slept the rest of the night before having to get up for work. It was a man's voice and his first words were, "I want to f**k you so bad." He went on to describe what might be a fantasy of what body parts turned him on, ending his message with what else he would like to do to me sexually. Did I just receive an obscene phone call? It was about a 30-second message and I felt disgusted. I listened again, my disbelief not allowing me to take this in.

Did I know this person? I didn't think so but I had an inkling of doubt. A name did come into my head but it was just a fleeting thought, sounds kind of like ... but no way, it was pure speculation. I saved the message and tried to put it out of my mind for the night. What could I do anyway? Don't these kind of people only get a thrill from the response of a live person on the receiving end of the phone?

I told a friend I'd been with the night before about this call and she said she would've been totally freaked out. Was I? I was disturbed but more into questioning why, and whether this was a random call. What if it wasn't?

I decided to play the message to an acquaintance at work who specializes in geographic profiling and threat assessment. She observed that although it was graphically sexual in nature, it was not threatening and did not make any reference specific to me. She also said that he sounded drunk and that the thrill for the caller can also be had in leaving a message. They didn't necessarily need to have a live responder to fuel their fantasy. Nonetheless, I was advised to be more attentive to my surroundings and let those around me know what was going on so they too could look out on my behalf. This of course would apply if the call was not random.

Although somewhat relieved with this assessment, I couldn't shake the feeling that I recognized something in the tone of the voice. The man that came into my mind, with hesitation I might add, is someone that I'd initially met briefly through work, maybe nearing ten years ago. Within the previous two months, I made his acquaintance maybe three or four times, always in a group social setting while out having drinks with our respective friends. Our conversation was friendly but minimal, and because we worked in the same field, he was someone I felt an implied trust with. After all, the man I'm speaking of is a police officer.

To try to determine whether this might be him, I phoned his work number to hear his voice mail greeting with the hope of eliminating him from my mind. I compared it with the message left at my home and asked a close friend to listen with me. She too agreed, it sounded 'like' the same person. And look what I'm in process of writing about? Is there some reason why this is happening now and if there is, what is it?

I don't have the answer to that question, nor do I know what to do about this call in this moment. If the voice could be verified, it wouldn't be random for sure. I've chosen to let some time unfold before I decide on how I would like to respond.

But what about the timing of this?

I have had some recent changes in my life, with regard in particular to a new presence of men in my life but no one has reflected anything like the deviant nature of the person who made this call. It does make me think about past relationships though, and the disparity of experiences and feelings they have brought and triggered within me.

Relationships

I have been feeling more open and optimistic about having a relationship lately, maybe in part because of the changes which have introduced me to a new social circle. I've been in this place before but it's been a while so maybe this time will be different. At least this is what I tell myself. In the past, despite initial feelings of optimism at the beginning of a potential love relationship, I would feel an undercurrent, an uneasy stirring that it was only a matter of time before it would come to an end. It would begin as a faint presence, and would grow stronger depending upon the demand on me emotionally.

How much did I have to allow that other person in, in order to have an intimate and long term relationship?

The truth is, I've never really gone there. I've sabotaged or disappeared emotionally, becoming invisible in a way. You wouldn't really know that about me, I didn't even know within myself how much I had been hiding out. Such is the nature of abuse, causing frailty of the emotional body that lingers like an old demon, hidden in the shadows of shame, only to rise up when it's existence is threatened. And when love comes calling, that threat can feel monumental, like light being shone on the devil.

Since it's been a few years since my last relationship I thought I'd overcome some of these old demons. After all, my intellect has given me the ability to articulate my past experiences and as time has gone by, I've continued to learn about myself. But this type of learning has done little to quell the disturbing reactions I've felt erupt when I've least expected them, and I've been shocked to see that they are still there.

It's a dichotomy really. I can be confident, self assured, intelligent, compassionate and understanding just to name a few descriptors, as told by my friends. I am generally lighthearted and fun spirited, focusing on the positive side of life. What still can be triggered from within me however are feelings of lack of self worth, guilt, shame, self loathing, anger and insecurity. And worst of all, that sense of paralysis to do anything about it.

The dominant triggers for my self degradation have been men, but I've also seen this side of myself through other relationships, including family and friends. What I've learned from this is that 'people' are not causal in terms of what we feel, they just reflect back what is already within. A disturbing revelation when you don't like what you see but also freeing because ownership brings with it the power for change.

And getting rid of the external triggers, while it brings initial relief from pain, is only a temporary band-aid solution. If you really want to heal, you must be honest and go directly to the one relationship which determines the basis for all others; the one you have with yourself. For me, the negative aspects that have shown themselves in relation to men can happen particularly if there's sex. For example, as stated earlier, if the sexual attraction was not mutual on my part, having to say 'no' felt so uncomfortable that I would rather avoid even the possibility of being put in that position. For that reason, there's never been a lot of casual dating. And if I did feel sexually attracted to someone, it was often to those who were unavailable emotionally, so there was no pressure on me to surrender so that intimacy could unfold.

I wasn't aware on a conscious level that I was in avoidance so it would just look like I was attracting all the wrong kind of men. Some were married or on the rebound from recent separations or just the 'player' type guys who I knew I could never trust. If I did act against my better judgment, for only harm comes from these involvements, I could detach from my body and have the sex without emotional involvement but in truth, found it to be a lonely and superficial experience. It was just not me and it actually fed the negative self image that was within me.

Having said all of this, if there was no sexual component, being friends with men has come easily for me and I have felt the protective nature of what some men have offered me through their friendship. And since I've worked in predominantly male environments such as law enforcement, and have for many years, this has been a very good thing. When I've talked of this writing to some of my male friends, several have asked if they could read it. And generally speaking, their feedback and reaction has been similar in that they are saddened by the emotional toll on me, the child, and greatly angered by the acts of the men who are cited in this story.

One of my old school friends who I've known since I was in grade five said he felt so sorry for what I'd gone through, even feeling badly that he hadn't known as he might have been able to make a difference in some way. My God, he was just a child himself. It reminds me of why it's so important for us to learn to be able to talk about whatever is going on in our lives, and obviously, the younger we are when we do this, the better.

Life Altering Change

Beginning in 2007, and within an eighteen month period, I had a change of work, the passing of my parents and a move to a new location. My mom, who suffered from Alzheimer's, had been in a care home for just over a month when my father died suddenly, alone in their town home. Even though he had visited my mom in the home everyday, she only asked where he was once, about three weeks after he had died.

She didn't seem to notice his absence. Although I spent many years barely able to speak to my father out of anger for his verbal assaults, I had by this time come to a different understanding.

My feelings of anger toward my dad turned to cool detachment as I became an adult. Eventually, I was able to separate the act from the person, I hated his act but I didn't hate him. In the week before my dad died, he asked me three different times to run small errands that he normally did himself, up to the day of the night he passed which was a Saturday. He had previously never asked me to help with these routine matters, and in fact he sometimes resented it when I would take it upon myself to do his laundry or help clean the house, so this was very out of character.

As it turned out, because of other commitments, I wasn't available to do these things for him but my sister was so I didn't worry, at least not until the Sunday morning. I had called him and received no answer which was highly unusual. My sister lived close to my parents' home so I asked if she would go and check on him, I felt that something was wrong.

My sister went and found our father on his bedroom floor, he had collapsed and died in the night. I felt sorry for my sister having to experience finding him like this and I felt sad that he had died alone, with no family around him.

It was very different for my mom who passed away in the care home five months later, with my brother, sister, niece and I at her bedside. I held her hand, and I swear I felt a little flutter in my heart in the moment that she took her last breath. My parents had good intentions and did their best, given their own struggles and challenges in life. By the time they passed, the roles had been reversed in terms of who was looking after who, as does happen so often with elderly parents and children.

Any dependence on them for support, particularly emotionally, had been replaced by my concerns for their comfort and well being.

A couple of years after my parents had died, I decided to have a reading from a psychic named Martin, who receives information from spirit guides who are with each one of us. In relation to my father, and without knowing any details from me, he said that my father knew at some level he was going to be passing about a week before he did. The calls for me to run the errands were his attempt to say good-bye but it was just not meant to be.

A greater loss, in terms of emotional support for me, came a month after my mom had died, with the passing of Dawn, who at that time I had known and learned from for over twenty-two years. As a teacher, she taught me many things, most importantly, to know that all the answers I might seek in life were within, and she taught me how to access that knowing. She was unconditional in her love and support for me, and lived with the greatest integrity of self that I've ever seen in a person.

She also had a wonderful sense of humor and was in many ways like a best girlfriend, so much fun! I've been blessed to have had her in my life, along with all the other experiences that our association brought. So, with her passing, as well as my parents, these changes were major.

It did cause me to stop and take a look at my own life, questioning where I've been, and what it's all been about? To see what I didn't have, and wondering what I needed to do to create what I would want now. It was like starting a new internal review. And sometimes to get the answers, it required delving into the past.

No real rhyme or reason on how far back to go, or to what events, except as how I was guided by the thoughts and feelings that surfaced as I looked inward and forward to see what this new future could bring.

It brought to mind what I'd heard once about what might happen if you're looking for love in your life. You may first be shown all the 'barriers' you hold within yourself against receiving it, and then you need to be prepared to face the reasons why those barriers are there.

In other words, the answers are not always as direct as we might anticipate or want them to be. Nor are the ways and means of how we might receive those answers, which too can be a process that is virtually impossible to predict.

Connection To Pre-School Abuse

The new work that I referred to taking in 2007, was within the Major Crime Section of the RCMP.

It was a nine to five position which was considerably less stressful than my work of the previous six years, in projects that utilized wiretap. That work was very interesting, always unpredictable but invariably demanding in terms of the time I was required to be there. No concern for me while in it but for some reason I was being guided to move on. I couldn't have known that within a year and a half of making that change I would experience all of the life altering events such as previously described.

This administrative work, also closer to my parent's town home, and the care home my mom eventually went to, had obvious benefits in terms of coping with all that had occurred. Was there something else for me to learn though, through the work itself? And if so, what could it be?

A few months later I would receive the answer through one of the files I was reviewing. Major Crime is a unit that investigates offenses which range from thefts and fraud, to sexual assaults and murder. The child exploitation cases, including those involving child pornography were for me, the most disturbing. And while always disturbing for the heinous and sad nature of the details, the effect upon me didn't usually stick, I didn't carry them home in other words. Whether it's desensitization through exposure, or my long time ability to compartmentalize, I feel compassion and empathy in the moment but am able to clear it from my mind in the next.

After reviewing hundreds of files, this becomes my norm, so to feel overwhelmingly shocked and shaken by the content I've read was totally unexpected. It was like that involuntary physical reaction that happened years ago in Carmel which was an awakening to knowing that 'something' had happened to me pre-school, that did involve a man, woman and another naked little girl. No other pictures nor recall of anything specific came to the surface, sexually or emotionally.

Memory can be that way, non-existent by all accounts until it is jolted to the forefront of the mind through the descriptive experience of another which is what happened now, at this time. *Intense* does not describe my reaction to this one particular file.

It was a thundering tremor that started at my feet and rolled right through my body. I was reading about forced and deviant sexual acts against a child that in truth shook me to my core. And I knew my inability to distance myself came out of my first hand knowledge of being a victim or witness to the existence of such abuse. I never talk about the sexual or physical details of these files that I read nor will I now.

It serves no one to disclose the nature of the sexual acts that are performed against children except for the purpose of prosecuting the offender or for the healing of the victim.

For me, since I'd never expose myself voluntarily to any material relating to such despicable acts, a police file reporting an offense of a child sexual assault would be the only way I would come across such an account. It took me a long time to come to terms with the remembrance this file triggered, but I was obviously ready to let it in, at some level. But how did I come to be reading this file which was instrumental in bringing, what feels like now, to be the final piece of this memory forward. All I really know is that many times, my desire to know truth and love, has been all I've had to guide me to where I've needed to go to learn. This appears to be the case now. I couldn't have planned it on my own.

So what was it about my pre-school abuse that made it so difficult to remember and piece together besides the obvious physical trauma? What was the emotional fallout? The answer to that question came in part while writing this story. In addition to the file I read that triggered a more detailed remembrance, I was re-listening to a recording of my chart which was done in the 1990's by an astrologer named Diane.

In one of our meetings, Diane had focused on when I was around three. She asked whether, at the age of three, I had any knowledge or memory of what might have happened then.

At the time I said no, not really having any pre-school recall. She further said that it appeared that something very traumatic left me with a tremendous sorrow that I was unable to share. I carried emotional feelings but they were basically pre-verbal so I never learned how to express what I experienced at the time. She also said I was 'part of" something, not in the sense that I was responsible, because someone else was, but I took on the blame. It would have caused a later shyness, like I was trying to become 'invisible.' She said, 'too much for a little soul to handle'. I didn't see it then but, my God, I see it now.

I actually believed that the little girl who was with me, the naked little girl, with that man and woman, was there because of me. I will never know more than this, or how and why it was revealed to me so clearly in this moment, but it's as if I'd been part of an ultimate betrayal, like leading a lamb to the slaughter. No wonder I couldn't take this in.

Can you imagine, especially from a child's point of view, what this would lead you to think about who you were? To be released now, through this new awareness, of an underlying belief that I was fundamentally evil and responsible for dark deeds that were committed, is quite frankly overwhelming.

This is the basis for the dark undercurrent; the feeling that though something might appear to be good, I need to proceed with trepidation, justified or not. Even to my work on Olson where intuitively, I was able to be in the right place, right time, but why? I would never have said it then, but secretly, I wondered all those years back whether my 'knowing' was in part because I was at some level 'evil' like him.

That's also why I didn't talk about packing that overnight kit when we did surveillance on him, I was again afraid it would say something bad about me. It saddens me deeply that the child within me would have carried this around for all of these years. It's also the key to why this memory has been so vague, difficult to access and without a doubt, the most emotionally damaging.

I've seen it many times before, through the files I've read, where children have been used to entice and lure other children but I just could not take it in, not in relation to myself. It's another integral part of grooming children for the purpose of sexual exploitation. As an abused child, if this too was how you were used, you are just as much a victim and utterly powerless to do anything about it. Predators use children like this, and out of innocence and fear they comply.

It can result in massive amounts of guilt, confusion and anger in relation to defining future self worth and ability to trust, to say nothing of the shame. And more than ability to trust, the effect for me has been in my reactions to those who have betrayed my trust. Trust, for me, is one of the most precious gifts you can give to someone, to entrust them with who you are as a person.

Perhaps because of the abuse of trust when I was most vulnerable, even as an adult I don't forgive easily if my trust is betrayed, especially with those who were close to me. And even with those I only knew from a distance, betrayal of trust could occur, without any kind of reason or warning.

As in the next chapter where this happened, coming totally out of the blue.

Out Of The Blue

Before I became a police officer I worked in a residential treatment home with emotionally disturbed children. I only worked there for a year but it felt like five because of extremely long hours and exposure to much more than I was ready for. I loved working with the kids but felt myself burning out. At twenty-one, I was hardly prepared for so much intensity. It was about a year after I'd left that job that I received the phone call. It was out of the blue, and was from a man I'd previously worked with in the same treatment home. I will call him Tim.

He wasn't staff in the traditional sense, he was actually more of a volunteer, having been a resident as a teen, a former kid in treatment. He was my age, and came back from time to time to help out with the kids. His six-foot-two build went a long way to discourage any potential violent outbursts from the kids that were in care. I had no personal connection with this man and I never saw him outside of work except one time while I was still working at the home, we'd gone for pizza after our shift.

To receive this call now was strange to say the least. He asked if I wanted to go to a movie. I told him, no thanks, I already had plans. He sounded drunk and when I asked if he'd been drinking, he said yes. Trying to be polite, I asked a few more questions about how he was doing before I told him I needed to go, because I was going out with the two girlfriends I shared a house with. I thought that was to be the end of my contact with him but I was wrong.

The house we lived in had two levels, with a separate suite on the ground floor, which we found out later was how he got in. My two friends and I had been out for the evening but when the break-in occurred, we were all home, in our respective bedrooms upstairs. When I first heard the screaming, I thought it was part of a dream I was having. As I woke up, I realized it was coming from just outside my door, from the direction of my friend's bedroom that was straight across the hall from mine.

I ran out into the hall, running head first into my friend Darlene who'd also come out of her room at the same time. We both saw the back of a man as he bolted down the stairs toward the front door. Once out the door, he ran across the lawn and out of sight down the road. We called the police, they were en route immediately. Our friend, who'd been terrified, was still in her bed in her room.

She'd been awake when she heard someone go into the bathroom which was right beside her room at the end of the hall, also just outside my door. She could tell it was a man urinating, she was alarmed. The two men who lived in the suite downstairs weren't home, and besides, they'd never use our bathroom in the middle of the night like this. She heard him come into her room but kept her eyes closed. He stood at the end of her bed in the dark and used his lighter to try and see who was sleeping there. She heard the lighter click and saw the light in the room change. She still did not open her eyes.

He was then standing beside her bed, now sounding like he was taking his shoes off. Still with eyes shut, she moved in the bed thinking he might leave if he saw her stirring. He then sat on her bed, and the next thing she knew he was getting on top of her. She started to scream and he tried to shut her up by shoving the blanket in her mouth but she continued to struggle. And for reasons I thought I would never know, and didn't until the writing of this story, he gave up and decided to run out the door.

As I am writing this section, my friend Sharon, who is the victim here, called me on the phone. I couldn't believe she was calling me in this moment. We'd lost touch for a lot of years but in the last couple, have reconnected and do have periodic contact. She's a friend from elementary school and regardless of how much time passes, we seem to be able to pick up our conversations like we'd seen each other yesterday. It happens with a few of my long time friends, and it was no different now.

I told her what I was writing about and asked if she wanted to hear it, at the same time not wanting to upset her. She said yes, to read it to her because she'd dealt with it a long time ago. When I finished, she said that the only detail that I was missing was that when she started screaming, she was actually screaming out my name. She also wasn't sure why she'd done that. I had totally forgotten that, or maybe I just didn't take it in. It makes sense now that once he heard her screaming out, 'Susan', he realized he was attacking the wrong person and decided to run.

When the policeman arrived that night, I gave a description of what little I saw. He asked if I thought it was someone we knew. I said I didn't think so, but this guy Tim's name came to my mind so I told him that too. Although, how would he know where I lived? The police caught someone on the street a short distance away and for ID purposes, they drove him back by the house in the back of the police car. I confirmed that it was Tim, and also found out in that moment that he was known to police, a fact I didn't know while working with him.

He apparently had a history of sexual assaults and violence, but as child care workers we weren't privy to this information. I think that's because when he committed his offenses, he was not considered to be an adult so his past actions would've been part of a sealed record. I testified in court, and he got off with a minimal sentence. My friend wouldn't stay home by herself from then on, and moved out shortly after.

The window he climbed in through was in the basement suite which was rented by two police officer friends who, ironically, were both working that night. I felt so badly for what he'd put my friend through. I know he'd actually come looking for me and from his actions, we can only assume to know his intention. Why did this happen as it did? Maybe this was a final push toward me making my decision to go into policing, but at the time it felt like just another event that was beyond my ability to reason with.

For certain, I seemed to have been protected once again but it wouldn't be the last time. Ironically, one of the next times that I found myself on the receiving end of unsolicited advances was a few years later, while I was working within the police force that I had been drawn to because of the sense of protection I thought it would bring me. For the most part it did serve me well in this way but like in most situations in life, there are exceptions to the rule.

Harassment

I'd been working in surveillance for a few years when I decided to take an extended holiday to Australia, where I was gone for almost three months. When I returned, one of my fellow team members told me that a bet had been placed on who I would be assigned to work with on my first day back. The joke apparently was that our team leader, who made up the list of who we would partner with on a daily basis, would put me with him because I was, after all, his little pet, one of his favorites. I was actually quite embarrassed to hear this. I was friendly with most people I worked with and my relationship with my team leader was no different than it was with anyone else, at least not from my point of view.

The last thing I wanted was any kind of special treatment so to hear of this little bet made me pay more attention to where this might be coming from. I decided to distance myself in whatever way I could so our contact would become as little as possible given he was my team leader and I had to work under his watch. The most I could do was minimize any time alone with him and, when in groups, insulate myself with the other people around me.

I had said nothing about altering my behavior so as to discourage being looked upon as his favorite, and it turned out I didn't have to. Almost immediately, the attitude of this team leader toward me became different. To make a long story short, over the following months he made my work life a living hell. He was constantly berating, demeaning and sarcastic in his exchanges with me, particularly in front of other police officers. His comments were always in the context of my work performance but I was competent in how I did my job so it became pretty obvious after a while that this was personal.

He would attempt to ostracize me from other members of the team as well, and did succeed with a few of them. And why would people go along? As I eventually came to see, his pattern was that while he would single out someone to favor, he at the same time had someone he was 'shitting' on, for lack of a better word. No one else would speak against him because they were just glad to be under his radar and didn't want to bring any attention to themselves. In private however, more than one person had whispered, 'I don't know how you come to work everyday.'

I didn't know how either, but after many months of taking his abuse, I decided to request a transfer from his team. In the RCMP, once you put 'paper in' on any given issue, it not only becomes a document that inevitably involves several levels of command, it tends to start wheels turning that you have no ability to stop. Knowing this, and despite how unhappy I had become at work, I didn't do this lightly. And before I submitted this paper, I went to this team leader to give him an opportunity to read what I was going to be handing in, and see if he could explain himself so we could find a different resolution, and perhaps avoid my submission to our supervisor.

He read my letter with a smirk on his face. He first admitted that he didn't have a problem with my work performance. No problem with that? So I asked, 'why the abusive treatment?' I remember him saying a couple of things in that meeting; he noticed that I'd changed where I'd sit when we had team meetings, that I was sitting farther away from him than I used to and he didn't like that. He also said I appeared to speak to and pay more attention to the other team members than I did to him. He singled out one man in particular.

Oh my god, this was more personal than I ever imagined. He was talking more like a jilted and jealous boyfriend, totally inappropriate given his role as my immediate work place supervisor. And again, I did not see this coming. He felt he'd done nothing wrong and so consequently, felt no need to apologize either. I then submitted my letter, first to our immediate supervisor who also tried to discourage it going forward. 'This letter is so personal,' I was told. 'We don't usually like to forward something like this'. That supervisor had no idea how personal a matter it was because I kept my reasons for wanting a transfer in the context of being harassed over work performance. I had said nothing of my team leader's disclosure of his real reasons for the harassment.

I was also afraid at that time that a dispute that involved the disclosure of such personal feelings on his part would then be considered a male vs. female matter, a point which would make it a sexually based complaint. I didn't want to be considered one of those women who couldn't cut it, working with the boys. This would just fuel the prevalent attitude at that time which questioned the wisdom of having women in this man's world anyway. I was transferred within the next couple of weeks and spent the next several years enjoying my work as I had done previous to having to work under this duress.

When I decided to leave the police force, I was given access to my personnel file which is where I read my supervisor's response to my request for transfer years earlier. He basically said that it was due to a personality issue between myself and this team leader, and that my inability to get along was the basis for the transfer which was granted. At the time, I remember feeling betrayed by these comments because it totally exonerated this bully from any wrong doing and put the onus on me in terms of being the cause of this 'problem'.

But I really couldn't fault my supervisor. My fear of being blamed in some way for my team leader's inappropriate behavior, to say nothing of the stigma associated with making such a complaint, kept me from being totally forthcoming. I know this was the case for most of the women he continued to harass and become sexually inappropriate with. Before someone with a higher authority took the matter seriously enough to take action against him, his behavior had gotten more extreme, and had gone on for years.

I'd been gone from my surveillance unit for several years when I received a call from the Internal section of the RCMP. They were calling with regard to the issue I'd had with this team leader years earlier. I was asked if my departure from the RCMP had anything to do with this man. I could honestly say that it did not, but why were they asking?

It turns out that further claims of sexual harassment had been made, leading to an internal investigation and subsequent criminal charges being laid. His career ended in disgrace and as far as the charges, he pled guilty to avoid a trial, and I believe, to spare his family from further embarrassment. He received a conditional sentence. Could this outcome have been different? I look at my own small part and wonder. I'm not sure if I was one of the first to file a complaint against him, but I know it took the silence of many to allow for his demise and the victimization of others to continue.

But it wasn't only the silence of victims that allowed this man's behavior to continue and escalate. It was also due to the 'he's just a good old boy, can't you take a joke' attitude that not only justified but encouraged his behavior, including his sexist remarks and innuendos. Considering a remark I got from another supervisor, it's no wonder.

It happened the day after I'd been on an afternoon shift surveillance, and we were just about to shut down for the night. Our target, unexpectedly started heading out of the local area, but the team, as a whole, was not authorized to follow him.

The lead investigator of the file however, who happened to be riding with me this night, requested that we continue. The rest of the team went home and we continued until we took the subject of our surveillance to a new address, about two hours out of town from our home base.

At work the next day, I was asked to explain to another supervisor why I alone was claiming overtime. I told him the circumstance, a pretty routine occurrence. As I was about to leave his office, I was asked, 'so, are you friends with him?' He was referring to the investigator I worked with the night before. I just looked at him. He repeated the question to me. 'Was he your friend?' I hardly knew the man actually so I said, not really. I thought to myself, what are you getting at?

The look on his face told me exactly what he was getting at when he said, 'Well, I guess if you weren't good friends on the way out of town, you were by the time you got back, eh?' I looked at him and said, 'yeah right'. He thought he had just said something funny to me.

I'm sure he didn't give his comment a second thought, but I did. It actually made me cringe inside, but I didn't let any of this show. There was no way I could even have conceived of challenging the inappropriateness of his comments. I certainly wasn't brave enough to take on what was, in essence part of the culture of being in this man's world that I had chosen to work in.

I know only too well how difficult it is to come forward with allegations of harassment or abuse, sexual or otherwise, especially when they occur in the workplace. And I for sure understand the resistance for doing so, because of the inevitable scrutiny that you come under, be it by yourself or those around you.

You are forced to self examine.

Follow Up To The Phone Call

Remember the obscene phone call I received after I had just started writing this book?

A few months have passed and there's been no further contact in this time. I have looked at my options as to how to reconcile this within myself and have come to the following decision. I don't feel like this was a random call as he had to listen to my voice mail recording before he left his message. In light of this, although I can't be certain, I'm not fearful that he's making these calls to others. I don't know why he chose me but do know I didn't personalize his action as I would have in the past.

It's 'not about me', it's 'about him'. I'm not responsible for his actions, nor am I to blame; something inside me is changing. As to his identity, I can only say that as I believe the sun will rise again tomorrow, I too believe I know this voice. As it stands, with this singular contact, I will take no further action at this time. It feels like the right approach for me and I trust that if there is something further to do, I will be guided toward that direction.

As far as including that he is a police officer, I do so for the following reasons. So often we hear and feel an expression of disbelief that certain people could be accused of sexually based offenses based upon who they are professionally. Whether they are a police officer, priest, teacher or coach, they are all people first, potentially vulnerable to being affected by all that can be experienced as part of this human condition. We learn to cope and sometimes compartmentalize, which can result in high achievement in one area and failure in another. Personal vs.

Professional, it is common that there is disparity in our ability to function in a healthy and balanced way.

For the victim, they too feel the pressure of not being believed because of the 'position' of someone who might be in their life, from family member to a person of authority. What we do and where we come from often has no bearing on who might become either a victim or an abuser. It goes without saying that trust by children in the adults in their lives is paramount and for the majority, this trust is warranted and honored. It's just to have awareness that these external factors should have little or no bearing on who or what is believable or possible.

And while the status of who the abuser is in a victims life can and often does influence the degree of difficulty in coming forward, once disclosure is made, you are still left with the same need to understand why this happened to you.

You're not thinking about whether this person is a cop or a carpenter, and it really doesn't impact the degree of shame or self blame you carry, at least it didn't with me.

I wanted to understand why me, but not from the abusers reasoning of why I was chosen for that would only serve to give them a voice to justify their acts. I needed to understand my circumstance by learning as much about myself as possible, especially from my past because of it's influence on today.

And since you can only learn so much through the limited recollections of yourself as a child, it made sense to me to pursue sources that could perhaps help me to further remember. Through the recommendation of a friend, I decided to go and have my astrological chart done. To be shown a connection between influences of my past and choices I made in the future was amazing and, in fact, serendipitous. But I could not deny the truth of what was being presented.

Connections Through The Chart

A personalized astrological chart is not comparable to those daily horoscopes you read in the paper as it is a much more detailed and precise accounting of your life based upon birth date and birth time. Even though it may seem like an unorthodox source of information, I know I was given unique insight and deeper understanding into reasons behind certain, and in fact, life altering decisions that I've made. Don't shoot the messenger, I say. Truth can come in many forms and when it shows itself, you know it.

Diane's method of determining what information might be relevant toward understanding my life was to zero in and find what she called anchor points, a connection between specific ages, feelings and events. She looks at childhood, to see if it appears that there is any influence in your current chart that relates to something from your past. In the couple of times I saw her, she spoke of many situations but I'll share only those that fit within the context of this story.

The focus was on when I was seven or eight. She said something happened there that made me feel less than, like I had been put down by someone, made to feel bad, perhaps by someone in authority. I told her about how I'd been picked up by the guy in the car. She then continued, well that influenced how you came to be doing something in 1981. What were you doing in 1981? When I told her of my work on a serial child killer she made an audible gasp.

It was like I had made a decision as a child that I would take this and other experiences and go toward the protective side for those who are most vulnerable. She also told me that my answers to her questions, which she'd prepared before I arrived, now gave her insight in terms of how to approach me with what else she had found in my chart. This was due to the disturbing nature of some of the things she'd seen in my history. At the time she had no idea just how right on she was, and nor did I.

Age Ten

Diane asked me about age ten, another time where something happened that influenced a decision I made toward the direction of my future. It would be like me making an internal promise in response to a circumstance where I'd said, 'no one would do that to me again'. She didn't always have details of what she saw in my chart, she only knew there was a reason why certain times were connected in terms of the past influencing the future, and why they were showing up now. She said, as that ten year old, experiences contributed to a choice I made when I was about twenty-two years old. I told her that was my age when I decided to go into law enforcement because it sounded interesting and kind of exciting. At least, those were my conscious thoughts.

The unconscious aspect of the decision I made was due to the molestation that happened to me at age ten, through someone known to my parents. Up until then, I'd told no one of this abuse. Who would have believed me? Parents commonly have friends who become like extended family, and when those friends also have children, access to each other is easy.

In my case, my parents were social so they often had parties where friends, and their children would come over on a Saturday night. As the evening progressed, after some drinking and dancing by the adults, all would be hungry so I'd help my mom make the late night snacks before being sent off to bed.

Most of their British friends made a fuss over the homemade fries that I was, by that age, good at serving up, and I didn't mind because like any kid, I wanted to stay up as late as possible. This was especially the case if there were other kids to play with, such as in these times I speak of now, where the son of one of those couples had also come to the house. He was a few years older than me, maybe early teens so this shy little pre-teen girl more or less ran away just by receiving a glance from him.

Eventually, when I was sent upstairs to bed, I would sometimes be leaving a party of music and dancing still happening downstairs. I would be just about asleep, or already sleeping, and would be awakened by him sitting on my bed. It was understandable, given the circumstances, that no one noticed his absence from downstairs. If he'd been caught in my room, he could say he was just saying good night, but it was really to lift my pyjamas and touch.

In response to my faint cry of 'don't', he would say, 'Shh, I'm not going to hurt you'. Then he would touch me down there. It didn't hurt but it made me feel sick and dirty, that same dirty feeling my dad's words would trigger years later when I was a teen and boys came more overtly into the picture.

This touching happened a few times over a relatively short period, maybe a few months, as I remember it. If only the same could be said for the residual emotional effect. It's not always obvious to those who are not predatory, but for those who are, even those who may still be in their teen years, vulnerability like mine can provide an inroad.

They can just sense it.

Age Eleven

At age eleven, despite the secrets I held within, I carried on like all was normal. I got decent grades, had lots of friends and was quite active in sports. I loved playing soccer, baseball and volleyball, the latter being my favorite. I was quite good at it, and was on the team that played in the inter-school competitions. My phys-ed teacher, and coach, who I will call Ms. K. also taught us in other classes. Although shy and terrified of being singled out, I was often scolded for talking in class and more than once sent out for laughing too much. It was a nervous thing really but it resulted in punishment nonetheless.

It was one of these times while in Ms. K's class where I was reprimanded for too much chatter with one of the boys. She called me 'boy crazy' and told me to come back for detention after school. She really didn't like me, at least that's what her anger in front of the class told me. While in detention, sitting alone with Ms. K, she started to talk to me. I was a little surprised at her friendliness because even as a coach, she was always rather stern and quite reserved. She never showed much of a softer side until this one day, when she had me by myself.

It was general conversation about friends and social activities, which led to talking about dancing and the new dance craze at the time. I can't remember now what that was. What I do remember is her asking me if I would be willing to show her some of these new dance steps. I was taken by surprise, not only because I'd thought she really didn't like me but also because of how weird it all felt. It got very awkward after that moment. I don't know if it was the look on my face or how else I responded, but the conversation and the detention ended.

The next time at volleyball practice, I learned there had been a change on the team. With no explanation, I'd been relegated to being a spare. She knew I really loved that game and she did have the power to include or exclude me. I wonder now whether that was her attempt to begin a grooming process with me, by using her position of authority to push me to wanting to get back in her favor. I was humiliated and confused but in truth it only fueled my own existing belief that said, 'you're not really good enough anyway'. I wasn't hard to knock down, I stayed silent and was never approached by her again.

If she'd ever been asked, she would probably say that nothing happened so no harm done, right? She would have been right in the physical sense but emotionally, this singular non-event from her perspective, had more negative impact for me than she could have cared to imagine. I thought of this teacher while watching an episode of Oprah where she was interviewing four previously convicted child molesters.

The Underline

One of the questions they were asked was how they believed their abuse affected the lives of their victims. One man said that he wondered whether what he'd done had actually killed the person that his victim 'could' have become. He hadn't murdered her physically because she was still alive but he questioned whether he had done so, in this other sense. I felt his sincerity and a deep sadness within myself at the same time.

Did this apply to my life with all that has happened? And what of this disparity between events from times past and present, remembered with love or for the lack of it. What other connection did I need to make? An excerpt from the books, 'A Course in Miracles,' came to mind:

"... and what could you not accept, if you but knew that everything that happens, all events, past, present and to come, are all gently planned by one whose only purpose is for your own good?"

In the past, these words brought me comfort and now, because of sharing their place in this story with a friend, I was led to a better understanding of their meaning and a surprise discovery.

It was over lunch with a friend that I spoke of this writing, with a general reference to the above noted quote. He was a Christian, and had not heard of 'A Course in Miracles' as his spiritual understanding was based primarily on the teachings of the Bible. The next day he left me a message on my phone saying that our conversation at lunch had prompted him to call.

He felt for some inexplicable reason that there was something in the Book of Romans (8) for me to read so he decided to phone and tell me so. His message also said that he didn't know if I even owned a bible, and he was right to wonder. I have been on a different spiritual path and the only bible I do own was given to me for my seventh birthday, signed and dated by my parents. I think my interest in Sunday school prompted them to do this.

I would go by myself to Sunday school in a church a block away from home, but maybe because I was so young, I found the teachings too scary. Floods and fires to contend with if you didn't do things right. In light of these reactions, I left the bible behind in terms of using it for guidance, but always kept it with my other books. When I retrieved the message about reading the Book of Romans, I was home having morning coffee with a girlfriend. I thought I would quickly look through the passage so I took the bible off the shelf while we were sitting, not realizing there were 39 verses to peruse.

I'll look later, I thought to myself, but just before I closed the book I noticed a verse was crookedly underlined in blue ink, in the Book of Romans. The verse was, "and we know that all things work together for good to them that love god, to them who are called according to his purpose". I haven't opened this bible since I was a child and now to be guided to this particular page, at this particular time was a little uncanny to say the least. Who did underline that passage, anyway? It showed me again how little we really do know about the grand design of things.

Understanding The Message

To receive virtually the same message, first from 'A Course in Miracles' and then from the bible, within a span of a couple of days, tells me that there is something in it that perhaps I'm not getting.

I have questioned whether I've lived to my potential or fallen short of what I was or am capable of because of the negative things that have happened in my life. I have wondered, are these negatives to be considered as setbacks and how influential have they been?

If I hadn't had these experiences, would my life be very different? Would I have had children, been married or on a completely different career path? I see with all of this questioning, that as much as I took comfort in the words I had read, I truly did not grasp nor embrace their meaning for me until now. As I re-visit my life from times past and present, through my conscious memory or remembrance triggered by the accounts of others, a different understanding has come to light.

How much of this has been a fulfilling of destiny?

Maybe it's the embracing of all that has happened that forms the basis upon which potential is achieved. And maybe it doesn't take away at all, but actually contributes in a positive way to what is possible.

When life events happen, especially those that represent the negative side of life, it's only human to want to forget them and move on. But we can also take these experiences and use them, not only to gain insight toward what we are here to learn, but to also discover more about our potential. Regardless of what we believe these life experiences represent or say about us when they happen.

If we embrace them all equally, a different understanding can unfold. Perhaps it's part of the grand design that, when the timing is right, based upon our willingness to ask the questions and our readiness to receive the answers, the feeling of needing to stay silent will be broken.

Understanding The Silence

Since this is my own story, I can only write from the little girl and the woman's perspective, I can't pretend to really know any other. What I am aware of however, is that when it comes to child sexual abuse and exploitation, the feelings of guilt and shame carried by victims are more alike than we know, regardless of gender.

We all share a common makeup of intellectual, emotional and sexual components, the sexual aspect I feel, being the least understood, especially in the aftermath of abuse. In the grooming process, with boys and girls, once the emotional bond is made, the physical aspect is then focused on.

Regardless of whether you understand what it means, when you are being physically touched and stimulated sexually, to respond is natural and may feel pleasurable. For most children, abilities to process what this means beyond what it is, do not exist. And that arousal, once initiated and felt, registers itself too in the body as memory and becomes associated to the emotional bond that has been established.

But what about when you begin to emotionally disconnect because your awareness is changing, and you see the truth of the violations that are being perpetrated against you. You're feeling emotionally repulsed, yet the body is still responding, and it can feel like a betrayal within yourself. And because it is not understood, and not talked about, you can easily be made to feel responsible for what has happened, and in some cases, continues to happen because of the shame taken on by yourself.

Abusers know this and play on it to keep their victims compliant.

If denial of these feelings happens instead of healing, it can also manifest as dysfunction in many ways, from promiscuity, addiction, self loathing, feelings of isolation and massive confusion around sexuality.

It's a heavy burden to carry as a child, I know that first hand from carrying around my own secrets. And the tragedy I'm finding is how many people, boys and girls, men and women, share the same story. How silence has long held these burdens in place, not to mention how it also allows perpetrators to continue to thrive in our society.

And I'm not naive, there will always be predators but our awareness of their existence and methods of operation will work toward diminishing their opportunities to act. It's time to open the flood gates, to communicate, and let silence in these matters be a thing of the past. And if you choose not to talk, at the very least it's to know that you aren't alone in your experience, your pain is understood and someone is there to listen when you are ready to share and be heard.

Change in Work

As I've written this story, I've felt an ongoing movement towards freedom from the emotional impact of what has happened in my life, and although intense at times, that intensity would subside, and I'd feel ready for what might be next. It's been an ongoing process of internal growth that has also been accompanied by new manifestations in my life.

I can't ignore what has been occurring in these past weeks and wonder at how all of the events are tied together. No intuitive warning signs of what might surface, nor order of intensity in terms of what I'm being shown about feelings that are still hidden within me. All I know for sure is, my life is looking a little different than it did when this ever unfolding journey of writing began.

On a professional level, my contract work for Major Crime came to a end. I'd been there for almost four years and really came to appreciate the dedication of the staff that worked under that umbrella, and the overwhelming need for their services. I felt this for the Integrated Child Exploitation (ICE) unit in particular. On one of my last days at work there I was speaking with one of the investigators who I'd become acquainted with. He asked me what I was going to be doing now.

I told him of my writing about the emotional fallout of child abuse, and he asked me, with slight hesitation, 'is it your story, did something happen to you'? I nodded and he looked at me with a hint of surprise and softness that I know comes from a compassionate understanding. He then told me of his own experience of an attempt to lure him, as a boy. He'd been playing in a park and was approached by a stranger who used the now common ruse of, 'do you want to see my puppy? It's

just over here in my van'. He said when he got to the van there was something about the way it looked inside that just didn't feel right, maybe something over the windows, so he ran.

He didn't know why he knew to run then, but he certainly understands through his current line of work what might have happened had he not. I know I too received some significant insights through the course of my work with that unit which perhaps was the real purpose in my being there. Not only to further healing from my own past, but taking that new awareness and utilizing it for the greater good. A way of acknowledging that saving grace that was also referred to in my chart.

Saving Grace

The astrology chart I received was apparently like only three others that this sage of a woman Diane had done in over forty years. She said that I had what was called, 'an exact trine', the meaning of which was lost on me. She further said that those other three charts were of Olympic athletes, and I didn't know whether to sit up straighter or cry.

I wondered, did I miss my potential? She explained, 'their level of achievement did not relate to the nature of their particular sport but to the level of their tenacity.' While my chart showed many positive influences, there was a darker side fraught with possibilities of date rapes, molestation, and other close calls but it was my high level of tenacity that helped me survive. This is what we had in common.

She said, 'you had to have been frightened or could have been stalked or had a sense of foreboding because you were a hair's width away from something like, danger, death?' 'Is this right'?

I nodded yes and had to agree, I've had some close calls for sure, to which she said the following: 'It was like the grace of God, the big hand in your back was there, that always just moved you out of the way. If you hadn't had those positive influences in your chart, that saving grace, such as you do, that could have been it.'

She continued, 'we can never be frivolous about that saving grace, like we're always protected no matter what. What this is more about is, that through your own transformation, taking vulnerabilities and turning them into strengths, you can help others.'

January 2011

Several times during the writing this story, I've gone from feeling complete in terms of the content of what I've shared to wondering if there was more. It seems to be a repetitive pattern I have. Just when I would think, 'I'm finished with that', I would come to realize that I was not. It was just before Christmas 2010 and I was in one of those, 'I think I'm finished' modes.

Now, into 2011, however, a couple of events happened that I feel compelled to mention.

One relates to my 'Age Eleven' section which involved my sixth grade phys-ed teacher. In retrospect, I'm lucky and feel fortunate that encounter did not materialize into another potentially devastating case of abuse, like what happened to some we know who come from the high profile, high stakes world of professional sports. As life, and timing would have it though, I had the opportunity to hear, and briefly meet one such individual.

His name is Sheldon Kennedy, former NHL hockey player, and he was the key note speaker at a youth forum which had been created by the youth and a dedicated group of policemen. I hadn't yet read Sheldon's book, and only knew through media coverage of his plight. He was here now to speak about it as a part of the forum that focused on child exploitation. I was invited to attend by one of the organizers so I decided to go.

I was truly moved by the way he expressed himself and shared his experience. He emanated sincerity, humility and compassionate understanding. I could see why he's had such an impact as the spokesperson he has become. In essence, he said that he'd never imagined as a young hockey player that he would come to represent victims of abuse but these were the cards he'd been given, and what really mattered in the long run is what you choose to do with the hand that you've been dealt. I can't imagine what it took for him to take the steps he did in the environment he was in, but I totally resonated with the outcome of his actions.

And I don't think it matters whether you're a former professional hockey player, or a former female police officer when it comes to the fallout of abuse. If the intent is to heal, the love behind that intention creates the bridge to dispelling any differences that keep us separate and unable to share. We find a collective common ground to stand upon, which I feel this man, so courageously and graciously, is contributing toward.

The other addition to the existing content of this story relates to the chapter 'Follow-up to the Phone Call' where I say that I'll leave 'as is' unless I feel guided to do something different. In the past few weeks, and seemingly out of the blue, this person's name has come up several times, just in casual conversation. I do have some acquaintances in common with this man, but he doesn't know that, and they have no idea who he is to me. One night after I had turned down an invitation to go out with this group of people, I learned later they had randomly met him and ended up being invited back to his home.

I felt myself cringe inside at the thought of actually running into him and this brought home the truth that I'm not as free as I thought from the effects of his actions. I've said that if I was able to get absolute confirmation that this 'is' who I think it is, he will be confronted and given an opportunity to explain himself. The truth is I don't need confirmation outside of my own knowing, in my heart I believe it's him. Where I was still affected was not so much because of the existence of the call but more because I allowed my own self doubt to prevail.

I won't seek him out but I don't feel afraid to approach him on the subject should the circumstance present itself. I wouldn't disclose that I had any physical evidence because that may be perceived as a threatening gesture on my part and perhaps would put my safety in jeopardy. For me it's not about exposing who this person is but more a case of holding him accountable which I know, if it's meant to be, I'll be given the opportunity to do so.

Personal Change

Since I finished my contract, I've not only had time to focus on this writing but have also been in the right place, right time to meet the person I've been seeing for the last few weeks.

His name is Patrick, and he's the first person that I've had a romantic relationship with since beginning this writing. Right from the start, we had a comfort with each other that would normally be the result of spending much more time together than we had, and when I introduced him as a former firefighter to a couple of my other firefighter friends, it was a little like bringing the brotherhood together. The level of comfort and openness I felt was only further enhanced with the implied trust that came through these common associations.

I think I can say our feelings in this way were mutual and yet at the same time surprising because it was so unexpected, for both of us. Of course I had my own reasons for feeling surprised and did wonder, what is this encounter going to bring? He's funny, kind, sensitive and attentive in how he is towards me. And while these traits are ones I like and find attractive, it doesn't explain my comfort and willingness to surrender and be open to sharing myself with him. Or receive what he has been willing to give of himself to me.

I feel more than a little exposed at this time, given the process I've been in while writing this story. And slightly insecure, due to all the unknowns that are in most areas of my life right now. In the past, these factors would have fueled an urge to resist getting involved but that hasn't yet been the case, which is part of what surprises me.

The other part of what surprises me is that I felt safe, not only safe but secure and cared for. I can't explain why, any more than I could explain why certain chemistry exists between people. After all, we have no history and haven't known each other long enough to even think about a future, but it was how I was feeling, at least when I was awake. When I went to sleep it was a whole different story, where a very scary range of emotions began playing themselves out, representing just the polar opposite to feeling safe or secure.

Dream Releasing

When I worked the Olson file, I was asked many times whether I'd been afraid, or felt that I was in danger? I can honestly say that on a conscious level I did not, and while engaged in surveillance was too focused on other details to let any fear enter in.

I did however, within a few months of his arrest, have a dream about him that did shake me from my sleep. In my dream, I was walking down an alley behind a house that we believed he was in. I was working as a police officer so I was strolling by to see if I could see any movement through the window.

As I was passing the backyard of the house, he came out and looked at me, making eye contact. In that moment, something frightening happened. I saw in his eyes that he knew, he knew that I recognized and saw the darkness of the devil that he was. He started chasing me because my knowing was now a threat so I began to run. I awoke from the dream but never forgot it, and I believe I had the dream when I did because I felt 'safe' to do so. He would never be able to harm me in any way whatsoever so I could re-visit through my dreams, the fear that I had actually felt while in his presence.

I mention this dream now because of several recent ones that carried the same feeling of fear I have just described. It was within a couple of weeks of first meeting Patrick that they started, and their occurrence would last over several days. They were nightmares really, and the fear is more aptly described as terror. I couldn't even take a nap without a nightmare being involved.

In one such dream I was walking away from a house I'd been in. It was dark and I had to walk along a sidewalk before crossing the street to my car. A man was walking toward me, all dressed in black and wearing a hood. He acted like I wasn't there, no acknowledgment whatsoever as he passed. Once by me however, the energy that hit me was terror. I felt he was going to chase me and kill me. I started to run and as I did, I heard him running after me. I was trying to get to my car and drive away.

As dreams go, my fright was so great that I woke up before he could reach me.

The last nightmare I had over these several nights had one distinctive difference. While all the others ended in me running for what felt like my life, the last one did not. I was walking alone when up ahead I saw a group of people whose attention was focused on something other than me. It was an isolated area, like on the bank of a river where there was nothing around but a bunch of trees. It was daylight, but I felt that familiar rumbling of fear start to surface as I saw they'd all stopped what they were doing and were now just watching me come toward them.

I didn't trust that they weren't going to hurt me so my knee jerk reaction was to run but something inside said 'don't', so I listened to the voice and walked on by. As they watched me come nearer, I returned their curious gaze.

As I passed, they went back to what they were doing and that was it, I felt free as my fear just seemed to disappear into thin air. It was that simple, I faced it and it was gone.

The meaning and nature of these dreams didn't make any sense at first, given the reality of recent events in my life. Consciously, I've been enjoying the company of this man and feeling an unusual level of trust in him, yet what is surfacing, albeit through my dreams, were feelings of danger, fright and wanting to run.

Was this some kind of premonition of what is to come or is it something surfacing out of my past? If it is old fears which are being brought forward, I am wholeheartedly wanting to be free of them, particularly since they are surfacing at this time.

Either way, the intensity of the dreams has gotten my attention and according to the outcome of the last one, if I'm to learn from the message, I need to face this in order to change it. Looking to dreams to find insight about life might seem unorthodox but so too is the way I've been taught when I 'journal' to find these same answers.

As I describe the process in the following chapter, you'll probably agree it's not a common or a well known practice, but it has been invaluable to me.

Asking For Assistance

As I've related earlier about what I received through Dawn, I was encouraged to go within when trying to understand what was happening in my life. In other words, I was being taught how to be my own authority in knowing that all the answers I needed were inside me. I learned how to focus and clear my mind so that I could receive insights and understanding in a different way than through the intellect or existing patterns of thought.

In this regard, I was shown how to write, not like the process of writing this book which in part is a collection of memories of events that have already happened, but to write whatever came to my mind once these memories are cleared. In the book, 'Zero Limits', written by Dr. Joe Vitale, an amazing Hawaiian man known as Dr. Hew Len describes two ways of living and expressing, either through the re-enactment of memory or out of inspiration, which you receive in the moment, from the Divine.

I know about writing from inspiration where I begin with nothing but a pen and paper to write down words that come, which sometimes are in response to a question I've asked. I asked now to know why these dreams were happening at this time. In part, I wrote the following in terms of these dreams and their meaning: The dreams you are having are those that are bringing forth aspects of your consciousness, re-creations of feelings that are there but not yet experienced in a way that facilitates their release.

The fear and vulnerability is in truth a remembrance of times past that had you trembling with fear. You are in a place now where you can cope with the feelings, in part because of the physical presence of one who cares for you and makes you feel safe. It is an example of what happens when you are open to having love in your life, for when you are open, you are open to all that is within you, including what you are in fear of. It does connect you to your past reasons for not letting love in and is a vehicle for you to use to bring forth that which has been buried yet needs now to be released.

A Perfect Storm

I don't know how the current events came together to create this perfect storm, bringing out what's most vulnerable in me, but I do know that it's happening. As I've been shown throughout this story, I haven't been aware of the weight of what I've been carrying from the past until it surfaces, often through unpredictable circumstances. These dreams seem to point to the existence of blocks that are still in place to receiving love, but now there's opportunity to bring down those barriers. I only know to start with what's happening emotionally at this time, where what's been triggered are thoughts and memories that I haven't had for years.

Over the past week, although I've had regular phone contact with Patrick, we haven't spent any time together. He had family matters to attend to, including an unexpected critical health condition affecting his son, so he was unavailable, and understandably so. At this time his son is in the hospital and while on the mend has a very long road to recovery ahead of him. This was the result of contracting a rare life threatening viral condition which rendered him temporarily unable to walk, a frightening situation for all the family to have gone through. And to put things in perspective, we've only known each other for over a month so on a priority level, in light of the gravity of these circumstances, our dating life would not be up there. At least, not in my way of thinking.

So why am I including this in my story? At this point in time it really has little to do with me or my life. I care about this man, and want to continue getting to know him but it's all still very new, and at this point only God knows what lies ahead. I only know that it all feels right today, in this moment. I trust in the fact that if it's meant to develop and become more than it is, that will happen too. Nothing to lose, right? That's how my mind rationalizes and for the most part, it's the truth of how I see it, however, it's not the full story.

While Patrick is in his life drama, my own roller coaster ride has been unfolding. I find myself dealing with old insecurities that have me thinking and feeling anything that would be remotely considered rational. Letting him into my life has brought back not only old memories of a past love, but also the devastation I felt when that relationship, which I'll speak of now, came to an end. I didn't know it then but the overwhelming feelings of lack of self worth and insecurity that I felt in that aftermath weren't caused by that breakup, but more a reflection of what were my own long held beliefs about my lack of worth as a loving, or lovable human being.

Love

I was in my mid twenties, and my boyfriend Chris was about the same age. We both worked in fields we loved, he as a firefighter and me, as a police officer. We shared many interests, spent most of our off time together and in general had a great relationship. I'm not saying this because I'm forgetting the bad stuff because there really wasn't any. We were friends before we dated so we'd already established an emotional connection. My parents and family loved him, as did my friends. In the few years that we were together he never stopped being able to make me laugh, he could reduce me to tears in a moment, tears of laughter that is.

You just have to picture a tall, dark and handsome firefighter of a man who, without warning, would start talking in a voice that matched the pitch of a six year old. He was very funny. I felt, as did those around me, that I couldn't have been in a better, stronger place in my life than I was at the time. That is of course until our break-up, which I didn't see coming, at all. Perhaps because of my level of awareness or lack of wanting to see what was going on, it came as a total surprise to me. But what caught me off guard even more so, was the intensity of how emotionally affected I was. I wasn't prepared for that.

I thought of myself as someone who had it all together, and I'd created a lifestyle that reflected this ideal. It can easily happen when you measure your life and who you are from the outside in. You build on appearances to make your life look to be a certain way, and you can even fool yourself into thinking that what you do, or what you have externally not only defines you, but also protects you. I was about to see how futile this way of thinking was, and how little control or understanding of myself, or my life, I actually did have.

Our break up back then wasn't long and drawn out, in fact it came out of the blue, and it was not based on a point I could argue. He said he just woke up one day and realized he didn't love me anymore, end of story. I was understandably hurt, as anyone would be but it was more than that. I'd wondered at times how I would feel if the relationship ever ended but I never anticipated the level of loss that I did feel when that became a reality, now that it was over. I'd been so careful to maintain my own independence, thinking that having family, friends, work that I loved, financial stability and other external factors would somehow protect me emotionally. Sleepless, anxious nights and affected work performance would tell me otherwise. I was coping but not in the way I was used to. My vulnerabilities were showing.

It didn't help that my parents had thought of him as a possible future son-in-law and responded to this break up like I'd wanted it and worse, caused it. My mom asked, 'what did you do?' as if I were to blame. I was already feeling like it was my fault. And his reasoning, which I interpreted as being, "because you're not lovable' could not have been more devastating to me, given my history. Although I had tried to create a self image for myself that said I was worthy and deserving of love, in but a moment that all came crashing down.

How can someone take that from you, or can they? At the time, it felt like something had been taken from me, but herein lies what I have just realized. It wasn't the loss of this relationship or Chris specifically that was so devastating, it was the belief that his opinion of me somehow determined whether I was worth loving or not. My value was completely dependent upon this person I'd opened myself up to, and my own sense of self worth was non-existent, determined by something outside of me, like I had no say in the matter.

Where was I in this equation? I didn't connect my feelings at the time of this break up with any childhood experiences of being controlled or overpowered but I'm beginning now to recognize a link. I also thought I'd gotten over the emotional impact of this past relationship but I see now, because of what is surfacing, I'd gone into denial. Back then, I felt like I'd fallen into a deep dark hole with no means of escape because the one who pushed me in was also the only one available to pull me out, and he was gone. And even if he was still there, how could I trust in him to help me, and not do me further harm. I was stuck, and out of survival I let the walls back up so I could cope.

Just like the child, I felt I had no means of escaping that emotional hell. Why would I? As a child, innocence, trust, and love was all I knew, and when that was taken, it felt soul destroying, like some precious part of me had been taken and was now gone forever. Re-connecting with the essence of who I was before the disconnect seemed impossible, too much to even think about.

Even as I grew into adulthood, that child became the inner child within me. I felt trapped. And that confusing cycle of thought kept me at arm's length from any desired closeness with anyone. Why am I seeing now what I didn't before and how did I come to a new awareness? In part, it's come about through this new relationship with Patrick, which may be, without knowing anything beyond today, one of the reasons for our coming together in the first place.

Reclaiming Essence

I don't know if there's a more sought after feeling when it comes to relationships than the one that happens in what is known as the 'honeymoon' period of a new romance. I know for myself it can be wonderful, and can only happen when you have two people with open hearts and minds, a necessary requirement if you're sincere in wanting to be in a relationship with each other. You have to allow yourself to be vulnerable, and you have to trust that this person has your best interest in mind, as you do theirs.

All easy when 'just happy to be together' and being 'on' with each other is the mutual feeling of the day, not so easy when the other realities of life challenge this state of bliss. But it's part of getting to know who this other person is, and whether in the face of all our other life pressures, we care enough to persevere. We're all the same in that we have our 'off' days, caused by our own internal thoughts, but what is different, is how we deal with what goes on inside us. Especially when something shuts us down, not only to ourselves but to those we would otherwise allow a connection with.

While I've been thoroughly enjoying the experience of this new relationship, old fears have been activated and felt, mostly through my dreams. I reasoned with myself that these were just old reactions because I'd had no experience of feeling disconnected from this man based on his actions and feelings toward me. I still felt vulnerable, but not afraid that this person could or would do anything to leave me with that familiar state of feeling less than, reduced in how I saw myself in relation to others and my value to them. I have to admit, I spoke too soon, and the knowing of this started intuitively.

We'd planned an evening together, particularly important to me as he was about to embark on a holiday, planned before I came on the scene. He was going out of a previous obligation, but nonetheless, he was going, and if I didn't see him this night, I wouldn't see him for several weeks. As the day wore on, my instincts told me that something was amiss. I was right, very uncomfortable but right. In short, he now didn't want to get together, he was having an 'off' day and would rather spend the evening alone. He said that I was welcome to come over but it really wasn't his preference because he wasn't feeling up to it.

This was a bit of an 'ouch' for me, as my automatic reaction was to feel offended and retreat but something told me that to persist would be in my better interest. Not an easy thing for me as I was already feeling defensive, on my way to shutting down in reaction to my perceived rejection of me by this one that I come to care so much about. In the past this would have immobilized me but not this night. I'm so grateful that I listened to that inner voice and went despite my initial resistance to doing so. All these details seem to me so elementary in the telling, at least to my intellectual self, but it feels necessary to include them because it's through some of these everyday, mundane situations that profound awareness can occur, like it did here with me.

It isn't my nature to impose myself, and I'm particularly sensitive about being in the company of those who 'want' to get together, as opposed to those who feel they 'should' based on a previous plan to do so. But here we were, together under those circumstances. He was gracious, but he wasn't having a good day. While I understood, I was also fighting my own tendency to let his influence effect me and bring me down. I contemplated running off home a few times, but, in the end, I made the decision to stay.

Once in bed, I couldn't go to sleep and feelings of sadness and loneliness started to creep into my consciousness. What was going on? As I lay there, I thought about my place down at the beach, and how full my life is with the love and friendships of the people who are now in it. New friends and old friends alike, my life is rich in that regard. I've given, I've received, and come to a new place of seeing my own worth. With these thoughts, I felt the truth of my own happiness come back, and that's when something hit me.

First of all, this person sleeping beside me isn't doing anything to me to make me feel lesser than. *I am*, he's only in his own process. In fact, the only one who can really make me feel less than is *me*. It's my choice in terms of what and how I want to think of myself and how I value my life, and it's how I value myself in a loving way that connects me to the love of others. If it's acknowledged, there's something to connect with and if I own it as mine, no one can take it away. I asked myself internally, 'but how do I stop being so affected by what he may or may not think of me?' Or any other person that I let into my life for that matter.

How do I overcome that influence in terms of my letting them make me feel small? The words that came to me were, 'it's your choice, it's always been your choice'. I realized then that what I was being taken back to was the experience of disconnecting, triggered by the abuse by those entrusted with my care. I've understood the abusers role as the trigger to disconnect but I'd never seen how I also believed I'd given them the sole power to bring me back.

What I'm realizing now is, even as that small child, it was my choice to shut down out of an instinctual need to survive. I did that myself and in truth gave nothing of myself away that could not be recovered. This doesn't mean I don't have to deal with the consequence of the experience, but it does change my perception of how the power was taken from me, and whether bringing it back to myself was in the hands of someone outside of me.

I don't know how I came now to this understanding at this level but here it was, and in this moment, in my body it felt like the weight of the world had been somehow lifted off my shoulders. It was a huge revelation for me, like I was reclaiming a core part of myself for the first time, equivalent to reconnecting to my own soul essence.

By morning, I felt peaceful within myself and so too was Patrick, back to being the light hearted person I was coming to know. I'm still not sure what the future has in store for either of us but I also felt in that moment, even if our relationship ended today, I couldn't have received a greater gift. I was grateful, back to feeling safe and secure in what I had with this person. A perfect place to be when you are about to be going off in different directions.

Unexpected Road Trip

After leaving Patrick on the last morning before his trip, I met with Kim, a woman I'd met through a mutual friend. And while our friendship was relatively new, it turned out we shared a common bond in relation to the effects of childhood trauma. She'd heard of my writing this story, so we decided to meet for lunch to further discuss these issues. I think we found a connection that comes when you have a true understanding of what another is sharing so needless to say, the get together was great.

As our lunch came to an end, the topic changed to what our plans were going to be for the weekend. Kim was going to Palm Springs with some friends, an idea which I must say suddenly sounded really appealing. Our conversation got me thinking, maybe I should take a trip myself. I'd been invited to go over the winter by a friend who'd recently bought a house in Palm Springs, but until now it had never felt like the right time. A few phone calls later, myself and my friend Cindy, who was also able to travel on a moments notice, were about to hit the road.

Two days later, we were driving to California, and would end up being gone for about ten days. I needed a break from my daily routine of writing, to say nothing of a needed reprieve from the winter and now cold spring weather, it was perfect timing. We were graciously received by Jim, my long-time friend from school, and then by Cindy's family, staying in both their homes for the week. A glorious week of nothing but fun in the sun around the pool, and in a manner of speaking, it was just what the doctor ordered.

On my return, before getting back into writing this story, I was asked by John, a young guy I know from the beach, how my writing was going. He's a twenty-something, and he told me he had just finished reading former NHL'er Theo Fleury's book, 'Playing with Fire', adding the general comment that he related to much of what was in the book. I didn't push for details but asked if I could borrow the book to read.

I read the book and it goes without saying that I could only feel empathy for the trauma Theo had endured. He was also a victim of Graham James, the same coach who had abused Sheldon Kennedy. I now felt compelled to buy Sheldon's book so I phoned the book store and they had one copy left. It was late in the afternoon when I got, 'Why I Didn't Say Anything' so my intent was to read it the next day. But as I lay awake at four in the morning, unable to sleep, I decided I would have a quick glance through.

I finished the book by eight thirty that same morning and was struck again by how I had resonated with all the feelings that Theo, and now Sheldon, have described. It also brought to mind a couple of other thoughts. I have only one male friend who's disclosed that he's a victim of sexual abuse but given the statistics, within my circle of friends and acquaintances, I'm sure there are more. This particular man that I'm speaking of also works in law enforcement, with the U.S. Government. It was after we'd known each other for some time, while sharing some of our history, that he told me that he too had been molested by a female friend of his mother. It happened when he was about six, he is now close to forty.

I'm not sure why he opened up to me when he did, I guess he knew by the little I shared with him that I would understand. I also saw his discomfort in talking about this, his embarrassment and confusion was visible. I tried to encourage him to explore how that was still affecting him but I don't think he was ready. We've been friends now for several years and he's never spoken again on the subject. He still chooses excessive alcohol use to cope. He's a high functioning alcoholic, and just like the hockey pros, he manages to maintain himself and perform his work to an above average standard, despite his inner turmoil.

I know he's like many others who carry around these secrets, and if I was a man in this world, I think I'd be overwhelmed just with the thought of who to go to or where to even start. I hope if there are others that I know who've had similar experiences, that they've been able to share their plight with someone, anyone who will give them support in becoming free of what I know is a very heavy emotional burden to carry.

The other thought that came to me was about how these two former hockey players have coped and maintained their continuing journey to wellness. When they hit their rock bottom, in order to climb out they had to be honest about their pain, and make a conscious choice to change their lives. In order to stay out of that hole, they have to continue to make their choices on a daily basis, not only in relation to their abstinence from substances but also in relation to the thoughts they have about their own self worth.

In addition, they both appear to have called upon something bigger than themselves for support which I too understand and relate to. It's like the saying, let go and let God … you can finish the sentence in whatever way you need to in any given moment. But why else would these books come to me at this time? And how did they tie in with what is unfolding on these pages?

On that last evening with Patrick, before going on our respective trips, I did find myself with a new appreciation of knowing the power of the choices we make. It's one of the common threads in these stories, but that somehow didn't feel like it was the complete picture.

Where was all of this leading?

I wouldn't get the other piece of that puzzle until I met again with Patrick, upon his return from being away.

Denial And Descension

After several weeks of not seeing each other, I was so looking forward to getting together, I've missed this person who I'd been having such a good time with. A few weeks earlier, we parted on the note that we would look forward to, and resume our getting to know each other, keeping our communication open to see what might unfold. We had this conversation because, like many new relationships, we come with our history and perhaps a certain degree of unfinished business that we may find ourselves having to deal with.

We say, okay, I have these things to take care of, but I want to continue having you in my life, so we'll work through these issues together. It's been my experience, when it comes to starting and continuing a new relationship, you need to at least be on the same page in this regard. It was my impression, before we parted to go on our respective trips, that we were. I seem to have been mistaken because, upon Patrick 's return, this was not the case.

All of a sudden, there's an unexpected withdrawal from this relationship, and a pushing away, from me. It's not my intent to expose anyone's private life so suffice it to say, because of his other life demands, he's now suggesting that perhaps until things get sorted out we should back off a bit. He felt I might have expectations that can't be fulfilled right now, so, he suggested maybe we should take a break. Didn't we just have a break? While I'm sure these words sound reasonable, for me they were totally unexpected and without reason.

I felt I was now considered to be dispensable, something which I had not felt from him before so my initial internal reaction was anything but reasonable. A kick in the stomach would have been easier to take. I really wasn't comfortable with how this made me feel but I didn't say too much because my fear which has now been triggered says, if you do he'll walk. He doesn't care enough about you to stay. And it's like an old voice inside agrees and says, of course he doesn't, why would he? In this negative state of mind, I didn't feel understanding, I felt discarded.

I couldn't believe I was thinking this way about myself, experiencing this old pattern of thought with an intensity that was totally unexpected yet in some ways should not be surprising. After all, in this process of writing I'm more open, have left myself more vulnerable than ever and have been asking for freedom from old fears and insecurities. But also in my discomfort and initial desire to escape from these feelings I made a choice that meant a denial of my own feelings in the name of accommodating his.

After a few days I began to realize that the suggestion to put myself in what felt like an 'on hold' position while this person sorts his life out was not working. I decided to remove myself from the mix, indefinitely. I felt initial relief and some sense of control but the truth is, any loving feelings towards him, or toward myself for that matter, were being replaced by feelings of negative judgment and regret.

What was I missing?

I say I felt discarded but it's been said, 'no one can make you feel or do anything to you, that you don't already feel or do to yourself'.

So when did I do this to myself? What began my descent into the negative hole that can become all encompassing? Does this happen when self love is taken out of the equation? I see now it was when I went into denial, a familiar old pattern again repeating itself. Obviously there was something more to learn.

My insecurities were triggered but instead of choosing to talk about that I retreated. Instead of speaking my truth and saying, I don't want to be a dispensable part of this relationship, in essence I kept silent. Truth be known, I was doing that to myself, making myself dispensable, discarding myself in lieu of another. I didn't trust that if this relationship is right for both of us, it will continue and grow.

I didn't want to lose all of the positive feelings I've had while in it, and out of fear of that potential loss, I felt myself starting to cling. I'd forgotten that those positive feelings, while brought forward through how we've been with each other, are already within me and not dependent upon anyone else in terms of their existence. I don't need to compromise my own value in order not to be alone, and I'm worthy of not settling for anything less.

And ultimately, if this relationship is purposeful for me, he'll continue to be a mirror for not only all that has been so good but also for what I might not want to see, yet still need to learn about. I haven't talked with Patrick about this yet, there hasn't been the opportunity. When there is, I'll share my thoughts and he can choose whether this is a relationship he'd like to continue in or not. For me it's clear, if we don't have a basis of truth in what we share, we really, in truth, share nothing.

Importance Of Sharing

In the middle of these latest emotional upheavals, I've felt among other things, sad, disconnected, irritated, and totally alone which I know comes from shutting myself down and not sharing while in such an intense state of self examination. It was depressing and sometimes totally consuming, resulting in sleepless nights. I couldn't stand being in this state which has not always been the case. To cut myself off from others because of the darkness I've felt when I've ventured into my own emotional mine field was many times the lesser evil. When you don't feel worthy, being open to receive love and intended support from others can be difficult because of what happens when one in denial faces one who is not.

But when you do choose to try to stay open to others during your own intense times, something else can happen because as diverse as we can all appear, we have much more in common than we'd imagine. In these past few months, I've been blessed with friends who seemed to appear at just the right time to help me find some clarity in whatever stage I was at in trying to get to a truth. Sometimes that came through their listening to me but it's also come through their sharing with me what they've experienced or have dealt with in their lives.

A friend who recently read this manuscript said she's felt so many of the feelings that I've described. She isn't a victim of sexual abuse but had her own experiences that have led to feelings of lack of self worth and insecurity. She's not alone, in fact as this story has unfolded, I've asked people, men and women alike for their feedback. In the majority of cases, it's led to a discussion of some aspect of what they too have carried around, excess emotional weight that's more often than not rooted in their childhood.

So many splintered people are just like me, trying to put pieces of themselves back together. And don't get me wrong, I don't draw a down and out crowd. They are for the most part, successful, professional people from all walks of life. But what they have in common, surprisingly for me, is their vulnerability and inability to express or truly understand why and what they feel.

I know certain people attach a stigma and often joke about what the idea of talking about 'feelings' means or says about us, particularly men who still think sharing themselves in this way reflects on their masculinity. Adversity can challenge all of us to see what we are truly made of, and to not have the ability to cope in this way when needed can sometimes lead to a tragic consequence when life presents us with the unexpected. This brings me back to Chris who I spoke of earlier.

Love Lost

When I began this story, I didn't imagine that I would be including the emotional fallout from my past relationship with Chris, the firefighter, nor any current relationship such as I have now with Patrick. But it is what surfaced and it felt right to talk about it. So too is what I'm going to continue to share about Chris. When I wrote of the relationship we had those many years back I had no intention of saying anything further, however, as has happened throughout this process, my dreams will sometimes push me in a direction that I wouldn't have thought to go. I had a dream about Chris last night, but when I woke up, I almost immediately forgot the dream but felt his presence as if he was sitting right beside me.

The dream was like a remembrance of what our relationship had become in the years that followed the end of our being a couple. It seems I need now to tell what ultimately happened after that break-up. Once I got over my own heartache, I was able to resume a friendship with him. We did have many friends in common and traveled in the same social circles so it was better for both of us to move forward amicably.

We didn't see each other often but we talked on the phone periodically, meeting for lunch once in a while too. One of the times when we met for lunch he spoke of the relationship he was in, this being several years after we had stopped dating.

Since I was his friend now, he confided in me that his girlfriend wanted to get married, but he didn't because he said he knew he didn't love her. I said, 'you need to let her go then'. He said, he didn't want to hurt her by telling her this. This was deja vu for me, I reminded him he'd done the same to me years before. He couldn't believe he'd done that to me, he'd actually forgotten. Funny how something so devastating to one, namely me, was hardly memorable to another. He did let her go and he never did marry. Maybe he would have, had his life not taken such a sudden and unexpected turn.

It was the beginning of December 2000 when I made a phone call to Chris. We had maintained our friendship for over twenty years by then and I had called mainly to invite him to my parents' 50th anniversary party. He was always a favorite of theirs and they would have loved the surprise of seeing him. We also spoke about other things, with him doing most of the talking. He rambled actually, like a person with a lot of nervous energy.

He touched on how he'd experienced some recent financial setbacks but didn't go into detail and I didn't want to pry. Besides, at the time, I was having my own financial crisis and chose not to share my circumstance because of the shame and embarrassment I was carrying in relation to myself. And, like many situations I've found myself in where I self judge, it feels like disclosure to others would only result in further negative criticism and judgment. So again, better to say nothing.

He didn't show up at my parents' anniversary party, and we never did speak again. I received a call on Sunday, February

4th, 2001 that Chris had died, that his body had been found in the water in Washington State. His car had been checked several days earlier by a local sheriff. It had been parked in a viewpoint pullout, beside a bridge in a scenic area called Deception Pass. It was absolutely devastating news to receive, he was only forty-six years old. And while understandably devastated I also felt affected beyond what I could reason with, an intense sadness bordering on despair that lingered for an unusual length of time, until I was successful at pushing it down.

After his death, I heard that he'd been suffering from depression and that he was under a great deal of financial pressure, something which I already knew in my heart to be true. And whether his death was accidental or deliberate, for no one was with him at the time, it was a certainty that he was not coping well when his life ended.

It's why, in retrospect, I've had regrets that I didn't talk more honestly to him about what had been happening with me. I know I'm not responsible for what happened to him, but I have wondered if it would've made a difference in how or what he might have seen his options to be, other than the ones that led him to drive alone, in the middle of winter and park beside that bridge.

This might seem like an extreme example to make the point about the importance of talking with each other but it is what it is. I didn't recognize it then but as I write about it now, I see that the intensity of feelings that were triggered by Chris's death were because I related to what he was going through, more than I was able to acknowledge at the time. And maybe in the telling of this, it will be meaningful or purposeful to someone else who may find themselves in a similar state of mind, namely that state of feeling so hopeless that the only solution you feel you have is the one that could potentially cost you your life.

Hopelessness

The sadness I felt at the time of Chris's death was understandable, but the degree to which I felt the despair in relation to the ending of his life was what took me by surprise. In truth, I'd never contemplated taking my own life and wouldn't have used the word 'hopeless' in how I viewed myself or the world so, what was I relating to? In hindsight, I think it was in how his financial circumstance was named as part of the cause of his despair, apart from the depression he'd been suffering from.

I hadn't known depression but I too had just experienced a financial crisis which was totally unexpected, and something I'd never anticipated would happen to me in my life. At the time I was in commission sales, and while I was able to build a business that sustained me for a few years, I was negatively affected by economic downturns in the real estate market. Consequently, that led to great financial hardship which brings me back to how I related so much to what Chris must have been feeling.

That financial hardship was a terrifying experience for me, triggering all of my insecurities and negative self judgments about who I was or what I was worth. The feelings in fact were no different than ones that were triggered by those who may have told me in their different ways that I was not good or lovable enough. But somehow this seemed worse because if financial loss happens in this society, it is often met with attitudes that deem you to be at fault and more deserving of blame than understanding. And if you were someone like me, who already held some of these views about myself, it was devastating.

For many, there is an association with self worth and finance, and judgment that your financial status is also what determines your value as a human being. I know I've held the same view in relation to myself, in part due to my conditioning. I remember when I was nearing graduation and talked about possibly going into social work as a career, my father's response would be, 'why would you do that, there's no money there', as if that was the only reason it would make it a respectable choice.

Even into my thirties, after I'd voluntarily left my work as a police officer, I was on the receiving end of slurs referencing my worth, or lack of it. Although I continued to work on a contract basis in the law enforcement field, I had also begun taking classes relating to self help and spiritual growth which also has a financial cost, like most forms of education do. It was also invaluable to me because of the friendships I formed with those who had the same pursuit, to better understand ourselves and this world we live in.

It was deemed worthless in my parents' eyes but I was happy and excited about my new path so in spite of their negative judgment, I still endeavored to share this journey with them. In retrospect, I believe it was my unconscious attempt to win their approval. My father's perception was that some of the new people in my life were wealthy, and because I wasn't, he thought and said the following, 'you don't have any money, why would they want to be with you, they're probably just using you'. Consequently, I stopped trying to explain, but it didn't stop the sting of his comments.

In May of 2001, a few months after Chris's passing, I was in New York visiting Dawn who by this time I had known for fifteen years. Dawn had been one of several people who had been negatively pre-judged by my parents when in truth she became my life long teacher and friend.

On that particular trip, while walking in Central Park by myself, I felt an incredible feeling of sadness come over me, which at the time I didn't really associate with anything specific, past, present or future. It was spontaneous, I didn't know where these feelings were coming from so I dismissed them and didn't try to reason any further.

When 9/11 happened a few months later, which also happens to be my birthday, I flashed back to that day in the park, wondering if I'd had some sort of premonition of that unimaginable future event. Maybe in part it was that, as I do sometimes have a sense of things to come, but as I look back now, I can also identify it as a feeling of despair. Initially triggered by Chris passing a few months before, that emotion surfaced again as I found myself in the midst of my own worsening financial crisis.

Is it more difficult to cope if the trigger for your feelings of lack of self worth are based upon financial loss? In some ways it feels like it is, for the following reason. While I can talk now about all my insecurities and feelings of lack of self worth and doubt that were triggered in my past, it was something I wasn't ready to do at the time.

Those were aspects within me that were my secret, and the thought of exposing myself in this way was in truth what was terrifying. When you are financially vulnerable, or are at risk of losing your home or job or other external circumstance that could threaten your well-being, it can in fact lead to nothing less than despair. If you yourself are not ready to face or cope with these unwanted changes, any way out becomes better than that alternative, even if it leads to the extreme.

And if you don't realize that your lack of self worth is not caused by a lack of funds, but triggered to come forward by unfortunate circumstances, you can easily continue to feel this desperation. Even to potential employers, it can feel impossible to reach out because your confidence is not there to do so. If you become stuck in this belief that lack of money equals lack of worth, it can lead to a sense of worthlessness that you feel unable to change unless your financial situation changes. That too can feel like a hopeless alternative, especially when you can't see the potential the future might hold.

While I was taken out of the cycle through the start of another career, I was still left with a nagging question of why it happened in the first place, like 'what did I do to deserve that?' After all, I wasn't a bad person, was I? From some within my family, I was treated like I was. No compassion or empathy for being on the receiving end of financial adversity. This was only worsened by an assumed and implied right to spew angrily at me like I had done something criminal, whether we were discussing financial matters or not.

The details of who and what was said doesn't matter now, but I include it to help bring awareness to those who may find themselves in the same circumstance, or may know of someone who is. They need understanding, not judgment, and just because the catalyst is money, it doesn't change what it can bring forth. Regardless of the cause, it's the same in terms of the potential emotional cost, and people need to be dealt with in a sensitive and compassionate manner.

Self righteousness, because you believe it would never happen to you, or the assumed right to treat someone with disrespect is not what a person needs when they are faced with an unexpected, and seemingly insurmountable situation. It's not what I needed but when in survival mode, like I was at the time, I didn't have the energy or feel I had the right to fight back, particularly against the anger that was expressed toward me.

Permission To Get Angry

I haven't always fully understood the impact of what I felt internally about myself, consciously or not, and the role it played in what I created, especially financially. In talking about it now, as with much I have shared in this story, recounting the past has been intense but also brings with it a sense of relief that comes from the process of letting go. And although this brings reprieve from the tension I've felt, and I've received new insights, the peace I experience has been fleeting. I'll find myself feeling agitated but not seeing my own part nor understanding why.

As I do once in a while when I have questions such as this, I'll pick a card from my 'Course in Miracles' set. The card I picked in this instance said the following: 'Think not you understand anything until you pass the test of perfect peace, for peace and understanding go together and can never be found alone'. So what am I missing in the throws of these latest changes and upheavals? If I pay attention to my own inner thoughts and see what comes to mind through recent conversation with friends, I see that what I'm missing relates to my tendency to invalidate myself in the course of trying to be understanding of others.

When I followed the feelings that come with these thoughts, what surfaced were long since forgotten memories of altercations with my parents, my mom usually being a reluctant witness. Whenever tensions would rise between my father and I, and I'd feel pushed to defend myself, or sometimes my mom, the scene would typically escalate into an angry, sometimes 'fist in my face' yelling match.

My mom would typically begin to cry because she couldn't cope and that was her way of diverting the fighting. As soon as she started crying, my father's immediate reaction was to turn to me and say, 'now look what you've done!', like it was my fault that my mother was crying. They would align with each other, and the argument would be over, until the next time. The message was clear, when I was upset, I upset everyone around me. That would trigger my guilt, not only for making my mom cry but for being angry in the first place.

For me to show anger was not acceptable, ever, so better to just keep my mouth shut to keep the peace. I was expected to be strong, keep things together. At least that was how I saw my role with my family, from a very young age. I felt responsible and this dynamic continued throughout my life with my parents. Even to when I was in my thirties, and their relationship was rocky because of my father's treatment of my mom. She gave my father an ultimatum to go and get professional help or she would leave. I had no idea what kind of help she thought he needed.

He did go alone to a therapist, and when I asked my mom what the outcome of that was, in essence I was told that his problems, their problems, stemmed in part because his oldest daughter, that being me, was not getting along with him. This is what my mom told me he disclosed to the therapist and it seemed to be acceptable reasoning for both of them. In other words, if I would just behave differently, and be nicer to him, things would be better. Of course, I wasn't the reason for his abusive behavior towards my mom, but they were in agreement, and she never spoke again of leaving.

This way of 'solving a problem' by talking around the people you should be talking directly to, as in my father going to my mother instead of me, rarely results in any kind of resolution unless it goes beyond this initial step. If you don't go right to the source, what you have is a dynamic that I call the 'energy of agreement' which seeks out support from others to strengthen how 'right' we are in our negative view and judgment of another.

And if you want to be 'right', you have to make someone else 'wrong' so nothing ever truly gets cleared. It is a common way of approaching issues, I've done it myself, and have witnessed it many times in others. I now know that this method of communicating breeds more contempt than understanding and leaves an undercurrent of doubt in relation to the issue of who you can really trust. At least, this is how it affected me.

On the surface, I went along with my parents' view of what would resolve our issues, trying to make an effort to at least be cordial but the truth is, I just felt betrayed. My relationship with my mom had changed, after all, I had been her protection and confidante. I had been her ally for many years when it came to my dad, because I was stronger, and I felt I had to be. I had taken that on and now it was me against them. At least, that's how I saw it.

The old message I carried was reinforced, it was not only unacceptable to feel or show anger, it was unacceptable regardless of what was being done to me or how I was being treated. If I did let the anger surface, it would also trigger the emotional cycle of guilt and responsibility for creating the havoc. It was the same cycle I'd already lived with for years so it was easier to push it down. What's the missing piece I'm seeing now?

It has to do with allowing myself, giving myself permission to get mad and accepting the feeling of being angry, particularly when relationships change from being healthy and loving to something less than, regardless of the many forms and extremes that can take. How do you ask someone to look at how they're affecting you when you don't feel you have the right to question their treatment of you? Especially when that treatment goes from respect to disregard, regardless of the severity of it?

In my way of coping, what was also missing was my ability to hold someone else accountable because of my feeling of being at fault for any negative outcomes. When you feel this way, the only place your anger goes is ultimately inward, leaving others who are responsible outside of the circle of accountability. Because of this, and for my own self preservation, it was easier to minimize a person's bad behavior and the effect it may have had on me.

And because I never went to that angry place with someone I really cared about, being too insecure to do that, blaming outside of myself didn't often happen. When it did, while blaming might have brought temporary relief from feeling angry it ultimately didn't provide any real answers as to why something happened in the first place. Nor did it provide any insight as to how it could be different in the future.

When you have been treated in a certain way by someone, particularly if it's been negative, it's natural to blame and look to them to know 'why'. But if they don't know or are unwilling to share that information, where do you go in order to find relief from the pain and influence of their bad behavior. Blame can provide a certain relief but still cannot provide you with any real understanding of why you are reacting to any situation as you do. Particularly if your reactions as an adult are rooted in childhood, which has so often been the case with me.

Limitation Of Blame

When I was around five, my mom decided to take in a little foster baby, whose name was Barbara. My younger sister wasn't born yet so there was just my brother and I and now this little baby. We all loved her, particularly my mom who, when I think about it now, could never get enough when there were babies around. One day, we were all in the car on our way to a picnic. My parents were in the front, Barbara and I were in the back seat, and my brother was in the very rear of the little station wagon we had at that time. This was long before the days of child seats or mandatory seat belts.

We had just started out. I was sitting behind my mom and Barbara was wrapped in blankets laying on the seat beside me. All of sudden, my dad had to hit the brakes and before I knew it, the baby had rolled onto the floor. I panicked and she started screaming. It all happened so fast and the next thing I knew, they were shouting at me. I didn't really know what was happening. 'Why weren't you more careful in watching her?' they yelled. I was horrified and just wanted to disappear. What did I do to the baby?

It turned out that she wasn't hurt, but for a moment I thought that she was and took on the blame. It's all bigger than life when you're that small, and so is the impact these relatively small incidents can make. I know it was probably my parents' own guilt that made them lash out, as well as their fear about what could potentially have happened to Barbara, but none of that reasoning mattered in the moment.

And it doesn't change the long term emotional imprint, especially if it becomes a pattern that is repeated and reinforced throughout the years. Barbara did stay with us for over a year, and I only remember my mom being absolutely heart broken when she had to give her up. She said she would never take in a foster child again because it was too hard to let them go, and we never did.

Of course my parents didn't know at the time that their own five year old girl had already experienced trauma in her life and they most certainly didn't have any understanding of the emotional duality I still carried by the time I was a thirty something. Yes, I was now an adult, but I sometimes brought with me emotional responses that were rooted in my past, from events that had happened throughout my childhood.

We were like many ordinary families in how we were treated and raised, I just happened to have had some extraordinary experiences that were beyond what most people imagine could be happening in a child's life.

Whether it's my parents, siblings, friends, or anyone else who has played a part in my life, they know what they know and they act accordingly. I do the same. So does it make sense for me to hold continued blame toward someone for their lack of awareness or understanding of me, or subsequent treatment of me based on who they think I am, but don't really know? And if I'm uncomfortable with whatever is happening to me, isn't it up to me to say so, and take my own action, accordingly? Wouldn't it serve me, and others, to take responsibility for myself to the best of my ability, when I'm able? I feel blame can have a place as an initial step toward healing but I don't see it as the end goal. Experience has shown me too, that it's not where true freedom lies.

Truth And Consequence

Over the years, I've had several readings from those who work in the metaphysical realm, from psychics who read tarot cards and such, to those who channel information from spirit guides or people who are no longer physically here.

I'm naturally curious about these communications, and enjoy hearing about the unique perspectives that come from those who can delve into past lives or look into the future to see what might be ahead. No way to validate or prove the information source except for how intuitively true it feels.

Besides, needing to know how or where information comes from is not essential for me since it's been my intuition that has often guided me to what is right or true. And I can't prove where that comes from in terms of its source, whether it was seeing through the stories of the 'street smart' teens I worked with when I was a young and naive child care worker, or knowing which way to turn while driving in surveillance. My inner guidance was all I had to lead me toward where I needed to be, and I couldn't begin to explain how that process worked, I just knew that it did and that I could trust in it.

On the subject of seers, one such woman I had a reading from was named Michaela, who would actually go into a trance-like state to channel information, something that I hadn't seen before, or since for that matter. Even with my open mind, it was a little strange to witness her method of relaying information, but again, not to shoot the messenger, I listened and felt the truth of what she was saying, as it applied to me.

In part, she said that one of my major life lessons this time around was to learn to stand my own ground, and not be a follower. I had apparently stood my ground in past cycles and got crucified for doing so, in a manner of speaking. Out of that memory, and fear of future negative repercussions, I became like the majority and followed the status quo, whether I agreed with it or not. This life was to be different. She repeatedly said, 'you need to follow your truth, and not be like the sheep, regardless of how difficult'. I must say, I could relate to what she was saying.

I've been almost obsessive about getting to know the truth in any matter, within myself or others. So much so that I also assumed that everyone would understand this pursuit, and want it as much as I did. Of course now I know, if truth meets denial, which most of us carry to varying degrees, it's like trying to mix oil and water, it just does not happen. And instead of being met with openness or understanding, it's met with resistance. And it doesn't matter whether you're addressing truth as it relates only to your life, it pushes in others what they may not want to see in their own.

I speak of this now because of what's happened as I've been in the process of writing and sharing this story. For the most part, it's been received with interest and support, but it's also been met with resistance, surprisingly by those closest to me which is where I get challenged. I've written this story because I felt compelled to do so, and that push is so strong, it's like I have no choice in the matter. I know too that it's a topic that can trigger a full range of feelings and reactions, some of which are involuntary and unexpected, not only for me, but for those who take these words in.

In response to the resistance, my old thought patterns about the benefits of keeping silent are surfacing, sounding something like, if you want to be liked, don't rock the boat or, if you want to please others and keep your existing relationships intact, just stay silent. People might not like what you have to say so be on the safe side, and say nothing. Old patterns of thought, based on past insecurities? Yes, but they are not without their influence today.

For example, I've experienced what seems to be a complete break with someone I considered to be one of my best friends.

And, coincidentally or not, that break started around the time I began sharing the initial draft of this story. We'd been close, having known each other and our families from the age of thirteen so it wasn't easy to see this change happening. It was gradual as our contact become less frequent and more superficial, to the point where there seemed to be nothing left to say. This was confirmed when I recently attended a high school reunion.

It had been months since we'd had any contact so the thought of possibly running into this former best friend did make me a little uncomfortable but I tried to put that thought out of my mind. What's meant to be will be, so no point worrying, right? The grad reunion was held at a hotel, with registration for the event being set up in the lobby, which is where people first began milling around. This is also adjacent to the elevators that led to the rooms upstairs and since I was staying at the hotel with other school friends, we made our entrance to the party from this point.

As the doors open onto the lobby, the first person I see and make eye contact is my friend, who happens to be standing right beside the elevator doors. I went into an automatic response of giving her a hug and saying something which I no longer recall. It was just in the moment, but within a few seconds, when the hug was over, there was nothing but the feeling of an invisible wall.

It was a little surreal, and then awkward, so I walked away and began to mingle. No further contact all night, it was like we'd never known each other. I've acknowledged her for all of her support over the years, and with sadness have come to accept that this may be the forever end of our friendship. So, do I stay true to myself or let the opinions or actions of those around me govern what I do or say? No simple question or accomplishment, especially when it comes to people you care about.

It can make the challenge of whether I do what feels right for me, or cater to the varying expectations of others a difficult one to deal with. Yet, as I speak my truth more freely, it's becoming less of an issue, altering the nature of my existing relationships and bringing a difference to who I currently draw into my life. And ironically in a way, the influence and judgement of others is becoming less important or influential.

I have support from friends who are new in my life, and from those who've been around for many years, and I appreciate them all. They help me see things sometimes when I don't have the clarity to see for myself. I know those closest to me mirror the changes I've been through, and the new friendships support forward movement and potential for the future.

And I know that letting go of what is known and familiar isn't always easy, but necessary. Particularly in these times when change is becoming the norm, not only individually but collectively as well. On an individual level, it can be that those who are known and familiar no longer represent what is best for you. A simple but clear example of this is what has to happen for the alcoholic who decides to claim back a life of sobriety. Their friends who drink may now represent temptation instead of the support that person needs in their decision to abstain so all ties may need to be broken.

It may be temporary or forever, but it's usually an essential initial step to take. The same principle applies when making inner changes in terms of how we want to be in our lives. When moving from being a victim of an influence, whether it be from what's in the bottle for those who are alcoholics, or from the negative effects of an abusive relationship. It involves not only changing from within but may also require creating new outer environments and support systems as well, as you're ready to do so. And sometimes, even when you feel you are not ready, it becomes necessary.

This might seem like a daunting task to undertake, but my experience is that with the decision to begin a journey of self discovery, to know my own truth, I've been assisted in some unexpected ways in creating these new and necessary paths. I'm led to people and places I've needed to be, and do seem to encounter those who also share the desire to understand how to be free within themselves, and out from under whatever might be a negative affect of some old emotional experience.

And it's only in retrospect sometimes that I see the relatedness of events, and how they all play out together to create what's in the future. It's even happened in the way this story has unfolded, topics that I couldn't have imagined would find their way onto these pages. Hockey again? Who would have known?

Stanley Cup Playoffs

When I completed the first draft of this story, it was post 2010 Olympics, a most magical time, not only for the city of Vancouver, but for Canada as a whole. Nationally, we were on an emotional high, and I think I can safely say for myself and others, we couldn't have been prouder to be Canadian. And to win the gold medal in hockey, that sport we claim as our own, was like icing on the cake. Canada against the USA, it couldn't get any better. Now I'm completing another draft, and we're into the Stanley Cup playoffs, another time where hockey is reflecting the emotional state of our culture.

So why am I bringing these hockey events into my story now? When I referred to the experiences of those individual players earlier in my story, I didn't anticipate that it would somehow link to these future entries. But in the aftermath of the final game of the series, I'm starting to see some kind of parallel between our personal stories of emotional fallout with what happened on the streets of Vancouver.

Just like during the Olympics when I'd received that obscene phone call those many months ago. It was surreal to receive that disturbing call, such contrast to the spirit of joy and goodwill that was prevalent at the time. It was Olympic hockey then, Stanley Cup Playoff hockey now, and that contrast of emotional acting out, increased willingness to express it, or inability to suppress it, is what got my attention. It gave new meaning to the words, 'prepare for the unexpected.' There's no telling what can happen on any given day.

I don't know if it's because of reading the books of Sheldon Kennedy or Theo Fleury but I have felt more emotionally connected to the sport than in the past. I was now looking at the league as more of a collection of individuals playing together, instead of a group of teams playing against each other. I sensed a vulnerability I didn't before and I'm more sensitive to them as human beings, beyond what they do as hockey players. Combine this view with the fact that the Vancouver Canucks were not only in the playoffs, but the finals, well, it was like the Olympics all over again.

The energy in the city was electric, and it really was a gift to have the opportunity to collectively come together to cheer on and support our hockey team. We were given weeks of being entertained and many times to celebrate and forget for a few hours all the things that worry us and sometimes make our lives mundane.

During the final series, I bantered back and forth via email and on the phone with a friend from Boston. He said that when he hears, 'Oh Canada', he thinks of it as a hockey song, not as the anthem for our country. I said, 'I guess that really means we own the game, no matter who wins, eh!' We laugh and say, no argument there. For me, this reflected the light-hearted nature of what the majority were experiencing, on both sides of the border.

Up until the final game, it was a roller coaster ride of hope, anticipation, sometimes disappointment, and celebration. I do remember looking with amazement at the thousands of people on the streets of Vancouver, and although a game might have been lost, all cleared with a relative calm, not unlike the days while hosting the Olympics. By this time I was looking at the whole event a little more deeply, it really wasn't just about hockey and the Stanley Cup but more about what it all represented in terms of who we are as a people, individually, collectively and emotionally.

Whether it's hockey for Canada, the Superbowl for America, or World Cup soccer for Europe, in the end it represents a common and uniting experience, which for the majority means promotion of goodwill and support for ourselves and for others. Beyond the sport itself, through the sportsmanship of the people, players and fans alike, it shows us our morality and in general, refers to virtues such as fairness, courage, and a sense of fellowship with one's competitors.

On a more interpersonal level, it also relates to the concept of treating others and being treated fairly, maintaining self control and respect for yourself and those around you, including those in authority or those with opposing views. What happened in the aftermath of the final game of the Stanley Cup series represented the polar opposite. An emotional acting out that is beyond relationship to any sport, and in complete contradiction to what is the inherent good nature of the majority.

In a word, it was devastating to see what exploded on the streets of Vancouver after the final game. It was a deliberate and planned display of emotionally unstable and violent behaviour by people who had destruction and chaos as their goal, regardless of who lost or won the game.

It was a mob mentality that caused personal injury to people as well as hundreds of thousands of dollars worth of destruction to property. Smashing store windows, looting, flipping cars and setting them on fire were just some of the crimes that were committed. And the people who were assaulted included some citizens who just happened to be in the wrong place at the wrong time.

Personally, I found it to be a heartbreaking scene to watch and yet I was angry at the same time, I felt ripped off. In a moment, all of the goodwill and reasons to celebrate were replaced by the occurrence of this senseless outburst. It felt overwhelming, and initially overshadowed all the camaraderie and fun that we'd experienced in the previous weeks.

I wanted to feel and remember my own positive experiences, but how do I do this once they've been displaced by events such as this? All I knew when I went to bed that night was that I wanted to get beyond the influence of all of the negative pictures and the feeling of being sickened by the actions of these few. How does this happen that so few can affect so many? My sense of national pride was replaced by a feeling of embarrassment and shame because of the behaviour of those who participated in this violence.

How do we move on from this experience and what are we to learn? I think the answers to these questions can be complex and varied, as are the ways in which people choose to heal themselves. Whether it's recovering from a bad relationship between two individuals, or moving beyond the negative affects of a collective experience such as this. But maybe it can start with positive action that may or may not seem associated to whatever event caused the disruption of peace in the first place. And it can be our own individual action that in it's own way contributes to the promotion of our goodwill as a collective.

Like, when you might find yourself in some unexpected trouble and you receive the assistance of a stranger, or vice versa. You reach out and help someone else despite perhaps being weighted down with problems of your own. These actions can take you out of a negative space and can initiate a flow back toward the peace of mind that we all seek. This happened for me, and it came through my interaction with something so small it fit in the palm of my hand.

Toward Healing

The morning after the riots, as I began to wake up I remembered what I'd seen the night before. I felt that sick feeling creep in again, initially not wanting to watch the news because I thought it would just be more of what had already been reported. I actually found it quite depressing because of the sense of powerlessness to undo all the damage, not only physically but in a spiritual sense as well. With a slight sense of resignation, I think about what can be done to right the situation but I don't really have any answers. In the meantime, I have errands to run so I decide to get ready, jump into my car and begin my day.

As I approached my car, which is parked in the underground of my building, I see something tiny moving on the ground behind it. As I get closer, I see it's a baby bird, fully formed but not feathered. It can't stand or fly and it's flailing around a little. My first thought is 'oh no, not again' because a few weeks before, the same had thing happened. I was walking toward my car and noticed something moving under it. I carefully backed up my car, and found a baby bird.

It must have fallen from one of the nests that exist in the ceiling of our garage, but I knew absolutely nothing about caring for these babies. At that time, all I could think to do was to gently move it, so I took a paper towel from my trunk, laid the baby bird on it, and placed it beside a post that bordered my parking spot so it wouldn't get run over. I didn't know what else I could do. I continued on with my day, leaving it on the ground, and when I returned from being out for about an hour, that baby bird had died.

Now on this first day after the riots, I find another baby bird? Maybe I'm just sensitive this way, but I found it heart breaking to find something so small and vulnerable and in such obvious distress. It's the theme of my day so far, feeling powerless, but I put those hockey related thoughts aside and focus on this baby bird, despite again feeling powerless to assist.

I don't know if they get pushed or fall from their nest, but they're too young to fly. I also don't know how they end up over to where my car is, since the nest is about thirty feet away, in a space between the ceiling and the foam-like insulation that covers it. As I kneel down to look closer, the little head lifts and the mouth opens, looking to be fed.

I can't bear looking at this, so I do as with the last. I pick it up with paper towel, move it beside the post, and leave to do my errand. Over an hour later, I return expecting it to have died, but again, the head lifts and the mouth opens. I feel I can't do anything so I head upstairs and try to forget about it. So much for out of sight, out of mind. I can't stop thinking about that little bird down in the cold garage. There must be something I can do?

I look online for sites on birds falling out of nests, not helpful because I really didn't know what kind of a bird it was. I then call a local pet store and to make a long story short, they connect me with a wildlife sanctuary. I spoke to a very kind man, frantically telling him the story of this baby bird who I think might die any minute. I ask, 'Is there anything I can do?' He says, 'you can bring it here'. I asked how I'd know it isn't too late to do that. He told me, 'touch the body, if he's still warm, he might have a chance'.

I thanked him and ran back downstairs, I was on a mission now. I felt the little body which was cold, but his mouth still opened and legs and wings were moving. It was at least a half hour drive to the sanctuary. What should I do? There's no way I could leave this now so with a Kleenex, into the palm of my hand the baby bird went, then carefully onto the passenger seat of my car. Still warm from running my errand, I hoped the heat in the car might help. While driving, I had to keep my hand cupped around him to protect him from flailing off the seat.

I was afraid he might break a wing, fall onto the floor or worse, get stuck between the seat and the console. I was pleading with this little bird the whole way, saying, please do not die. Talk about distracted driving, it was a pretty ridiculous sight in retrospect and it makes me laugh now in the telling of it. But at the time all I could think of was getting this bird to the sanctuary before it was too late.

It turned out it wasn't, we got there on time. The kind man who'd been on the phone with me earlier took him from my hand and told me that by the looks of it, he has a good chance of survival, they just needed to get him fed as soon as possible. On my way back home, I not only felt a sense of relief and satisfaction, but also a change in how I'd been feeling earlier that morning. In taking action with that little bird, and the ensuing positive outcome, a small sense of peaceful accomplishment began to override the heaviness I'd been feeling, related to the negative stories of the night before.

I found out later that this change of sentiment was also happening on the streets of Vancouver. And while that change was based on action of a much grander scale, unrelated to what had occurred in my life that morning, I saw an aspect that was parallel in the connection between taking action and the resulting transformation of feeling. It can move you from a sense of feeling powerless to make a difference, to seeing the positive results of the difference you can make.

What happened through the people in Vancouver was a more than amazing demonstration of the power of the collective. And because of what precipitated that positive action, I think it demonstrated something else we need to be paying attention to that relates to our sense of responsibility, or more accurately, 'our ability to respond'. Not only in understanding what happens within ourselves, but to know how to deal with what is happening.

Our individual thoughts and feelings do precede any action we take and whether good or bad, it does have a ripple effect. This was shown to us in spades when we witnessed the massive response to the violence that had taken place after the game.

Responsibility

With only the intention to right a wrong, an estimated fifteen thousand people, organized mainly through Facebook, headed into the downtown core volunteering to help clean up the devastation from the night before. I was so moved when I saw and heard what had come together, and felt in some ways it was an unprecedented example of the generosity of spirit that we have. Organizers worked respectfully with city officials and police on the impromptu plan to accommodate all the people who wanted to come downtown to volunteer, an event in itself that required a degree of trust from the authorities. And it's not 'that' we responded which was unprecedented for me, it was the attitude of 'how' we did so.

There was no time wasted and little talk of blame, only a clear and constructive intention to help clean up the mess. Not unusual when responding to devastation caused by accidental means or mother nature, but when it's the result of deliberate and clearly destructive violence by other human beings, it makes this response exemplary. So too was the response of those who found themselves in the middle of the violence as it was happening the night before.

Besides trying to protect property from the rioters, ordinary citizens put themselves at risk to come to the aid of people who had also been attacked in this mayhem. They suffered injury as well in trying to assist police in trying to bring some order to the chaos. Their actions were involuntary, triggering an innate willingness to protect and assist when called upon to do so, which brings me to another thought. What do we expect of those who, while living in one the most peaceful and protective nations in the world, act in ways that might only be justified if war, poverty and suppression were a way of life?

Really, what's the excuse for this out of control and violent behaviour? It's a disruption of peace that's certainly not justified in terms of the general environment we live in, nor did it have anything to do with being a hockey fan. So how do we respond to those who act out in these random and violent ways? Do we now have to restrict our freedom to gather, prohibit certain kinds of public events, increase security and police presence and hope that all goes well? Maybe it's the answer with respect to crowd control, but it doesn't address what's behind this eruption of chaos in the first place.

And in the broader sense, when you look at the aggression behind those actions, you see that we're still dealing with the fallout of unexpressed negative emotions, but of a different and more dangerous kind. It's anger, unexpressed and accumulated, and it explodes as violence and is projected onto whoever and whatever happens to be around. Indiscriminate and random, and done without any thought of consequence. Do we call it mob mentality?

It could be explained somewhat by that label but that only addresses a collective action and doesn't explain the behaviour as it relates to the individuals who make up the group as a whole. Consequently, there's no accountability. And without personal accountability, there's little chance for real change and new understanding to occur.

In this world, where change is becoming the constant, there seems to be something different required in order for us to understand that what is felt within us, left unexpressed, can and does contribute to the chaos around us. Since it appears we are so emotionally driven, perhaps we need to start there, not only in increasing our understanding of the role of emotion in our lives, but also by increasing our understanding of the effects of denying the expression of those emotions and the ensuing dangerous charge that it carries as well.

Consequence Of Denial

I looked up the word 'emotion,' and found the following definition: 'One of three fundamental properties of the human mind, the other two being volition, which is the exercise of our will, and the intellect.'

In my mind this leaves the emotional property playing a significant role in defining who we are. So what happens when we deny this feeling aspect of ourselves, and what are the consequences? In a collective and possibly in the worst sense, I think what I've written about in the last several chapters, is a good indicator of what can happen.

If in denial, we become unbalanced and whatever negative influence we carry can manifest into violence and severe physical harm, not only to ourselves but to others. But if we express our feelings instead of denying them, there's no cumulative effect nor intensity that can lead to what's out of control and unforeseen. Who of us hasn't experienced the feeling of relief in the body when we let go emotionally? Whether it's allowing yourself to cry when you're sad, or verbally expressing anger when you're mad, the effect is immediate and usually diffuses any further need or temptation to act out inappropriately.

And I know there's just as many different reasons as there are people as to why denying our truth has become more common than expressing it, but in taking steps to change this in our lives, we have to become aware and honour what is true for ourselves. It's essential if we want to move toward knowing our own potential to live in peace with ourselves and those around us. These reasons alone should motivate us to begin seeing the importance of the expression of what we feel, and the possible outcome when we do not.

And in the case where we internalize our denied negative feelings, instead of projecting them by acting out on others, the consequences, mentally and physically can be equally harmful. I know first hand about this because of what I spoke of earlier relating to the duality within my own consciousness. I drew 'bad' things to myself, even though I was in denial of the extent of the negative self image that I carried within myself.

My lack of self awareness didn't stop the bad things from happening, it just stopped me from seeing them coming and understanding why. Energetically, like draws like, and in this way I got what I 'thought' I deserved. Such is the consequence of denial, it didn't stop the negative influence of the self judgement I carried, but it did in its own way remove me from

116

having to consider why I manifested the experiences such as I did.

So what happens when we become aware of emotions that we've previously denied, through conscious choice or those involuntary triggers? How do we cope? Since what or who's around us can evoke what's within us, even what we would rather not experience, we commonly cope by controlling our environment. A simple example is how we spend more time with people we like and feel compatible with and minimal time with those who, as the saying goes, push our buttons. Like being with certain family members or with colleagues at work that, but for the obligation, we would otherwise avoid altogether.

We cope by controlling our time with them. So what happens when and if we don't have the same ability to control who or what's around us? What do we do when this external approach to controlling an internal conflict within us no longer works? Before the arrival of the Internet, it's a question we would hardly need to consider. Today, it's one we can't afford to ignore because of the unprecedented access into our lives, and multiple new electronic ways to communicate, whether we invite the communication or not.

For some, these methods have replaced direct communications, and are used to avoid having true and authentic exchanges with others, especially in matters that are personal. Who of us doesn't know someone, or have received ourselves, an email or text relating to a sensitive issue that should've been dealt with face to face because it's what would have been appropriate. Not only is it disrespectful but it is dismissive in that it denies the other person the right or ability to respond in a direct and more meaningful way, if they so choose to do so.

And while the technology has obvious benefits overall, it can also be a bombardment of information and communications that necessitates coming up with new ways of managing and coping. Social media and networking are also demanding in terms of the time and energy it takes to respond, even if the exchange is positive and invited. And when it is not, such as what happens with the shamefully common occurrence of cyber bullying, the resulting consequence can be extremely disturbing and sometimes tragic when the unsuspecting recipient does not yet have the needed skills or ability to cope.

We have much less control of the influences that come from the outside that inevitably trigger what's within, so our only real option is to better understand what's internal so we can respond and promote living in harmony with the world around us. It's like reversing how we've traditionally self managed, working from the inside out, moving from being reactive in our denial of ourselves, to being protected through our acceptance of who we are.

I also think it's the most effective way of minimizing the occurrence of unwanted experiences because by becoming more conscious of your own needs and doing what is positive and purposeful for yourself, you draw to yourself more of what supports you and less of what does not. But how do we reverse our thinking and start to see that we are our own best authority, and the answers that we need to promote understanding of ourselves are within.

How do we get there from here? Again, it is different for all, but I know for me it was a gradual learning over many years through many relationships. The next chapter describes a little about my process.

Change From Within

When I was growing up as a teenager, I loved music and the pop stars of the day, from the Eagles to Led Zeppelin. It was and still is a great source of joy in my life. I saw music as the great connector as well, because it could often take people beyond their individual differences to a shared common ground. Powerful enough to bridge generations, like between parents and kids or on a grander scale, connecting people from all over the world. The global influence was and is undeniable.

The Beatles 'All you need is Love' and John Lennon's 'Imagine' were prime examples of that, and also represented the kind of music that I related to most. I was after all growing up in an era of peace, love, rock and roll, it's what I understood. And while I was drawn to most songs like the two above, there was one artist's music that touched me in ways I really didn't understand when I was a teen, but somehow still felt a connection with.

It was the music of Canadian poet and singer/songwriter Leonard Cohen and today, as I am writing, the words from one of his songs came into my mind. They're from a song called Sisters of Mercy and the words that came were:

You, who must leave everything that you cannot control
It begins with your family, but soon, it comes 'round to your soul
I've been where you're hanging, I think I can see how you're pinned
When you're not feeling holy, your loneliness says that you sinned.

As a teen, I really didn't get their meaning in a way that I could articulate or consciously relate to, I just knew the song touched a sadness in me. In hindsight, they described a pattern of thought and belief I held that I now see in the following way. I carried negative feelings about myself that I felt powerless to change or control so I disconnected from them. I closed down and in doing so I felt a sense of being isolated from other parts of myself. You could liken it to feeling like an abandoned child, except it was the child within me and I'd done this to myself.

At first, the resulting isolation was preferable to the negative feelings I was trying to avoid. And in its own way, it brought relief and a self fulfilling punishment because in abandoning myself, I thought that isolation was what I deserved. Not only from myself, but from those around me. So when someone wanted to get close to me in an emotionally and physically intimate way, I would sabotage to stay in what was my comfort zone. How would I do this?

I'd take the uncomfortable feelings that were triggered within me, and project them onto who I was being pursued by. I'd find some fault with them that would justify why I went from feeling excited about a potential relationship with them, to utter distaste at the thought of being in their company. That's how I would distance myself and move on.

In retrospect, I had become quite a master at this projection, easily gaining the support and agreement of my friends who would understand and support my reasons for why this person was not good for me, whether their behavior warranted it or not. In truth, some did deserve much better consideration but they didn't have a chance because after all, I was in a protective mode with myself, and there wasn't much chance of getting past the wall I'd built up.

Although my process was somewhat internal, with the aim of pushing the pursuer away, it's not unlike the cycle that keeps many women staying in abusive relationships, in that it comes with its own form of twisted protection and isolation from self. It's often hard to fathom when looking from the outside why a person would stay in an abusive situation. And who in their right mind would endure that? It's not so hard to fathom if we understood that it might be because staying feels like a lesser evil than starting the process of leaving.

Sometimes looking at what got us in a situation in the first place is difficult to face, and easier to avoid, even if it means letting an abuse continue. My cycle of isolating only worked for me until I became more open to wanting to have an intimate relationship in my life. The isolation I had created as a protected place I could go to within myself began to change and I liken it to the following.

What once had the feeling of a cozy room I could walk in and out of at will, started to feel more like a room I'd get pushed into against my will because I wasn't wholly wanting to go there. I was now struggling with the duality within myself. This change happened as I became more self aware and self loving, and I wanted to overcome some of the negative patterns that had driven me for so much of my life. For a long time as an adult, I still continued to sabotage relationships, albeit unconsciously, but instead of the usual relief in feeling isolated, I began to feel the loneliness of it.

In not understanding my own role in the creation of those feelings, I thought that it was others who caused me to feel what I did, and I began equating not being in a relationship as punishment that happens to people who are not worthy of the desire or love of others. It's how I thought about myself. After all, look at what I did to myself. I had taken my negative self judgments and projected them on those who had any real interest in me. So what happened that turned this thinking around and brought it back to me?

It was a simple realization I had one day when thinking about how I felt when any relationship ended. It didn't matter how different the people were that I'd been involved with, or what the duration of the involvement would be. The common denominator was their interest in having an intimate relationship with me, and my resulting and seemingly inevitable feeling of distaste toward them. This usually marked the beginning of the end.

Even though the names and faces of the men changed, my residual feelings were always the same. That's when it struck me, if they were the cause of what I was left feeling inside, there would have been some qualitative difference as it related to my experience with each person but there never was. They weren't the cause of what I was left feeling inside, they were only the triggers to bringing forward what was already there. That was key to the beginning of my understanding that to change and deepen my connection with others, I needed to do the same with myself.

And why am I writing of this now?

All I know is that it's what came to mind when I asked the question, where to from here? And how does all of what I've written about relate to the emotional fallout of child abuse?

In part, it's because it doesn't matter what acts imprint themselves with memory of our feeling small or less than. What matters is recognition that we may still carry this limited image of self around. And with this awareness, and love of self, these patterns can be transformed and manifest as change for the future, including that which can be the unexpected.

Expect The Unexpected

I n the last few weeks, I'd set a goal for myself that I'd like to have the content of this story, apart from editing, completed by September 11, which as I stated earlier happens to be my birthday. It would be my gift to myself, and to that end, except for a final chapter, that goal was accomplished. As the weekend approached and subsequently passed however, there are new events that I feel now need to be included. As well as updates on certain aspects of what's already been recounted.

Several people who've read previous drafts of this story have asked, whatever happened to Patrick? I wish I had a definitive answer, the romantic optimist in me would've liked to have written something toward a happy ever after direction but it's not the case. I don't really know what happened with him. He's read this story, except for this chapter and he was supportive in my sharing what pertains to him.

We saw each other only a few times up until the middle of summer and while conversations became progressively more intimate and comfortable, without explanation, he stopped communicating.

So does this mean that those feelings of insecurity and bad dreams that manifested when we first met were in fact a warning sign of things to come, and not triggers from my past? I think maybe it's a little of both but in addition, although hurt by his actions, instead of feeling I was less than in the aftermath, I felt mostly a sense of loss in terms of what perhaps could've been. Those were wonderful feelings I felt while with him, and they're still within me, and perhaps meant to be shared with another.

Do I think of or want him to return? While I've decided to move on so to speak, I don't feel the door within me is completely shut in terms of letting him back in if that choice presents itself. But like all else that happens, you can only truly know what you might feel in the moment so best to try to stay open and see what lies ahead. Now to the morning of my birthday. My brother called, and the first thing he asked after wishing me 'Happy Birthday' was, did you hear the news?

I hadn't yet seen the news and my first thought was, oh no, did something bad happen relating to 9/11, after all, this was the 10th anniversary of the attacks in New York. Thank goodness, nothing to do with that 9/11 and everything to do with the safe return of a three year old boy named Keinan Hebert, who'd been abducted five days earlier. A 911 call was received in the early morning hours to inform police that he'd been returned, literally to his family home, by all accounts unharmed.

Given the expected and more common outcome of children never being seen alive again after stranger abductions, this was a miracle. Especially in light of the subsequent arrest and charge of the offender, a man with a criminal history which included previous sexual assaults against children. How did it culminate in this best case scenario? In addition to the Amber Alert, a press conference was held where the father, in essence, made a plea to the suspected abductor to please just return the child to a safe place.

He spoke a few simple words, possibly scripted by police, to appeal to the conscience of this obviously emotionally disturbed man. If the expertise of the experienced investigators was used in this regard, their approach was successful. I'm not privy to the inside workings of the case so what I'm saying is at best an educated guess. I don't think it's accidental that it was five days after his abduction, and only one day after the father's plea, that this little boy was returned.

Maybe it's because of my own story and work history but I was moved by this amazing news, enough to put the event in this book. As one police spokesperson said, this outcome was unprecedented and for sure, totally unexpected. Many 'unexpected' and 'unprecedented' events in the past few years, now marked by anniversary dates, have been negative reminders of man's inhumanity to man. Today, on this 9/11, this reason to celebrate represents the positive side of what's possible. And even though the numbers of people's lives affected doesn't compare, there's nothing small about the recovery and return of an innocent three-year-old child.

Later this same day, for my birthday dinner, I was taken to one of the beachfront restaurants I live minutes away from. After dinner, we'd planned to walk to the Westbeach, the 'Cheers' style bar & grill mentioned on the first pages of this story. As we'd finished our meal, my sister Tricia stepped outside the restaurant for a few minutes. When she returned to the table she told me some people were out on the street, calling my name. One of them had approached her, thinking at first that she was me, as we're similar in looks. My sister laughed because the woman who turned out to be a friend of mine, but not known to my sister, had looked so puzzled when she got close enough to see it wasn't actually me.

As I glanced out to the street from our booth, I recognized one of the people who'd been looking for me. They'd gotten tired of waiting at the 'Westbeach' and knew I was somewhere on the strip having dinner so they set out to find me. It was a hilarious and heart warming scene to have this group of eight pretty crazy acting adults show up in this way to say, 'Happy Birthday!' I love that kind of spontaneity!

One of the people in this group was Kim, the friend I'd connected with for lunch months before, just before the Palm Springs trip. She was here now, not only bearing gifts for me but proudly showing us the new engagement ring she had just received from Scott who was also with this gang who'd just walked in. What an incredible change for both of them, in less than a year.

And how is it they came together, ready now to receive a relationship which led to this engagement, when only a few months ago, it was a completely different story for both of them. I've quoted the saying before in this story, that 'love waits on welcome, not on time' and I think their coming together is a good example of just how true this can be.

Prior to meeting each other, they'd both had experiences that became catalysts for having to face the negative effects of childhood abuse. These emotions, ranging from lack of self worth to rage, now seemed to be feelings they were no longer able to deny or control. For Kim, it happened through a previous relationship, something we had spoken of during that time we'd met for lunch last spring. She had come to an awareness then that she still carried debilitating feelings that would potentially sabotage any possibility of having a healthy and intimate relationship. With purposeful intent, she began the process of freeing herself of these negative thought patterns. The success of that intent speaks for itself, in what is happening in her life today.

For Scott, who shared his story with me a few months before this day in September, the catalyst came through a last minute decision to make a trip home, to a place he'd moved away from twenty years earlier. He was from a small town, located about a seven hour drive north east of Vancouver. And while he'd been back every summer visiting and staying with friends, he'd never gone back in the winter to stay with his family. Now, as he told his story, it is three days before Christmas 2010, and he is about to arrive at the home of his sister.

As he was driving down the hill in the final approach into town, he found himself feeling a familiar swell of emotions which were involuntary, intense and totally consuming. Many different feelings but mostly anger, triggered now through the return to this location that held remembrances of what he'd also been thirty years on the run from. This happened every year as he drove down this hill for family visits, but he could push the feelings down. The diversion of friends and busy summer activities tended to shield and protect him from his thoughts and feelings, but unbeknownst to him this was not to be the case this time.

The focus of the anger he felt was towards his step-father and although no longer with his mother, he still lived in the area close to the family home where he grew up. When Scott got to his sister's house, he went in and tried to shake the anger of the childhood memories he was now being tormented by. He couldn't do it the same way he could when with his summer visits included staying with friends. There were triggers here that just fueled his anger, like what he felt when he saw his sister. He saw a great sadness in her that he hadn't seen before to this degree, and he knew it was rooted in their childhood. It just became unbearable for him to watch.

On Christmas day a few hours before dinner, he decided to leave the house, explaining he was going for a drive to visit some friends which consciously, he intended to do. When he got to his car and began to drive away though, something else happened. He found himself driving straight to the apartment building where his step-father now lived, parking outside in the lot. He sat thinking about ways he could cause grievous bodily harm to this man, he wanted to kill him.

After about two hours, his thoughts began to turn to the potential consequence of committing such an act, and the effect it would have on his life now. He decided to make another choice, and an hour later, he was arriving at the local police station. He walked in and said, 'I want to report the sexual assault of a child'. Scott, now forty-one years old, was that ten year old child that he was only now able to step up and defend. The young female constable, not yet understanding the urgency of this moment, suggested maybe he come back another day, after all it was Christmas.

When Scott responded by saying that they had to take a report or he was going to go and kill someone, it became a different story. He maybe shouldn't have said that, but it got her attention and it was what he was feeling. That day was the beginning of a process that months later resulted in several sexual assault charges being laid by crown counsel against his former step-father, not only for what happened to Scott, but to his brother and sister as well. Those court proceedings are ongoing, and the trial date is yet to be determined.

It was an incredibly brave decision for Scott to make, and certainly didn't come without its own fallout of doubt about the wisdom of his choice and the potential collateral damage to his mother and his siblings. In the ensuing months, thankfully he's had the support of his family, in addition to voluntarily seeking counseling to help with the process of healing. In that regard, and part of the reason why I've included these events, is what also happened after his having gone to the police.

Scott and I had also spoken about how he was in relationships, before and after his going forward to the police. He knew the same experience as myself in his aversion to intimacy. He couldn't share his experience, or receive the appropriate understanding with any previous girlfriends so he'd just disappear as a way of coping and getting out of the discomfort and back into the neutral zone.

As a part of his therapy, it was suggested that he return to some of those past relations to explain his actions. He said their feedback was that they understood and were in fact relieved and grateful that he'd told them the truth because in all instances, they thought that they'd done something wrong. Such is the emotional frailty of more people than we can imagine which leads me to another connection which surfaced, surprisingly I might add.

Scott is a scout for the Western Hockey League and had shared his story with a friend who also works in the hockey world. While still in the throws of wondering if he'd done the right thing, he received an unexpected phone call. It was from Theo Fleury who Scott had known from afar but had never personally met. Theo had heard about Scott's situation and called to offer his support, knowing all too well what Scott would be going through. While assistance and understanding had come in many forms, that one phone call was pivotal in that moment in terms of erasing any lingering doubt that he'd made the right decision in doing what he did in taking this court action.

After learning of Scott's experiences, I just have to shake my head in awe as to how small this world really is. My thoughts go back a few months to my meeting with Kim, my return from Palm Springs and being presented with Theo's book, and now meeting Scott who relates his story. If there's any doubt that there's a connection between all things that happen, which we might not see but for the daring to look, that doubt is not in my mind. There may not always be recognition or understanding of the links, but in the long run, and overall, I think they do exist.

In that regard, I feel compelled to include another real-time and unexpected event in this story. In the midst of working on another edit of these pages I heard on the news that Clifford Olson had died. Small relief for the families I know, in light of the forever loss of their children, but final in his removal from further appearance in their lives. My reaction also felt surreal for some reason, like a strange mixture of relief for the families, to a sense of wonder at the timing in relation to my being in the final stages of writing this book.

And then came the dreams ... the night I heard the news about his death. I went to sleep as usual, only to be awakened with a shudder, like being jolted awake by the noise of someone in your room when you were expecting no one to be there. Then I'd fall back to sleep, only to be awakened several more times in this way, like I was running from fright. I don't remember where I was in the dream but the feeling was that it was a dark and utterly evil place, and the name Olson was in my thoughts.

It was like I was being exposed to his energy, necessary for some reason, but I could only handle exposure to that darkness for a brief time, so I would be awakened to be protected. These dreams, like this writing as a whole have been cathartic, and leave me feeling like his death somehow is the manifestation of the end of an influence of darkness. With regard to the dark influences in my own life, it's like a purging has taken place, a 'removal from the position of influence'.

I hope that it's symbolic too of the finality of their influence, and absolute in any further ability to cause harm. I wish this too for the children of Olson who for some reason have come into my mind. I think of his son, a new born baby when he was sent to prison. He would now be thirty. I can't imagine having to live with Clifford Olson as an inescapable part of your own history. I've wondered if he knows who his father is or whether he's been raised as someone else's son. If he does have knowledge, I hope he also knows clearly and absolutely that his father's acts are not his burden to carry.

Unfinished Business

Little did I know when I was writing the previous few chapters how much I would need to listen to my own words, especially in allowing for the unexpected to unfold. During those real time writings in September 2011, I truly felt that I was complete in terms of my story's content and was ready to focus on promotion and publication.

So much for what we think we know! Subsequent to the time of those writings, life itself has again brought me to a new awareness of an experience previously recounted in my story. What I had once considered myself to be complete with, I now see as unfinished business.

It's about the obscene message left on my voice mail in 2010. When I initially enquired about my reporting options there did not appear to be any that would not take the complaint out of my hands and leave me outside of the loop in terms of how the matter would be handled. And because of this, in part at least, I had decided to let it be, unless I felt guided to do 'something' further.

As it turned out, 2012 brought that further guidance.

It was a year where the RCMP were in the headlines for all the wrong reasons. A class action suit was being filed against them, and other complaints of harassment, sexual and otherwise, put them in the news as well. Every time I would see a media piece on these issues, I would be reminded of the phone message I had received and wondered, albeit quietly to myself, should I have done something more?

Since I too was an employee at the time I received the call, I wondered if there would be any change in terms of the recourses available for the registering of complaints. There had only been a suggestion to me that it could be addressed under a process called 'code of conduct' which might result in a loss of pay or some other kind of ineffectual reprimand. I would not be included nor have the opportunity to attend when the person was presented with the allegations.

In my mind, my attendance was paramount because I wasn't seeking to do irrevocable damage to this person's reputation or career, I just wanted the opportunity to present what I had experienced and be a witness to their response. And regardless of their response, it would still be me they would have to face which is a big part of the accountability I was seeking. Since that option did not exist, my original decision to leave as is still stood and although not totally satisfying, seemed appropriate, that is until the following interactions took place.

I contacted the police officer who is assigned to what the RCMP had called the Respectful Workplace Action plan. I expressed my interest in knowing about potential changes that were going to be implemented in terms of handling and reporting incidences of harassment. And I felt that due to my own experiences I may have something positive to contribute, although I was not sure of the form that would take.

We exchanged a couple of emails, and eventually I asked if there was any possibility we could get together for an informal meeting. This led to a meeting with Carol, who generously and promptly responded to my request.

I can see why she was chosen to spearhead this daunting task. I found her to be open, compassionate and sincere in her manner, and I was grateful for the time that she had taken to meet with me.

I shared with Carol some of my background, and without identifying the person in my complaint, except that he was a police officer, I told her about the phone call I had received while writing this story. I also shared why I did not report it at the time, explaining that it was because there was no internal support system available where I would also be included in addressing the subject of the complaint directly, in the company of a third party, who would perhaps act as a mediator.

I said too that to have the choice of self representation, as opposed to not being involved at all, or being represented by a third party, was an extremely important option to have when considering whether to file a complaint. While I sensed that she agreed, it felt to me like it might be something to be considered in the future, but there was no option in place to utilize at this time.

We spoke briefly about consequences, and who would or should have any say, given a list of options, in what would be appropriate. What did become clear was that this process would only be feasible if the accused person admitted responsibility. But what if they did not? I did not anticipate the internal questions I was asking myself as I spoke with Carol, but it soon became clear that they were ones that I needed to know the answers to.

The first question in my mind was, in my circumstance, would I be willing to sit down with a mediator and confront him with this accusation? Yes, I would be willing to do that. The second question was, would I be willing to confront this man by myself? After all, if accountability to me is what I seek, then why would I let that be dependent on a third party being present, especially when it is clear in this moment there is not going to be one.

The next thing I found myself saying out loud was , 'I think I need to call this person myself, with or without a mediator.

Carol said, 'you're very brave.' I didn't feel brave, in fact it was in this moment that I realized it was my fear of confronting this person that allowed me to 'leave as is' based on the non existence of what I thought were any appropriate options.

By the end of my meeting with Carol, what I had previously thought I was done with was now feeling incomplete. I told her that I would be making the call, because of my need to satisfy my own integrity. I just needed to drum up the courage to do so. I did not disclose the identity of this person to her, it was not the reason I had asked her to meet with me. And in my view, would not have been appropriate. I did promise that I would keep her informed.

I knew full well that the final outcome of what I am taking on is unknown, and in part dependent upon the response or reaction I get from this man who is yet to know, but soon to find out, about my impending call. The very next day, I decided to call his work number and ended up having to leave a voice mail message. I basically identified myself, not sure but hoping he would recognize me by name as we have only ever been casual acquaintances. I said briefly that there was something I needed to speak with him about and asked that he call me on my cell phone when he had the opportunity.

One week later, I still had not received a response so I decided to try contacting him via email. Since it was Easter break, I felt if he was out of town he may have set an auto reply stating so, and that would at least give me some ease as to why he had not responded. In my email I explained that this was a follow-up to a phone message I had left on his work phone the week before. I again requested that he call me, saying only that I didn't want to be alarming or dramatic, but it was imperative for me that he do so.

Within twenty minutes of sending the email, I received the call. His tone was courteous, and he did appear to know who I was. He was in fact out of town, on vacation in the States. The call was short, and we only discussed the date he was coming home and his promise to contact me in the first week of April when he returned. He did call again as promised, and since it was a Friday, we only spoke of scheduling further contact once the weekend had passed and he was back to work.

I had asked about meeting at his office because I wanted somewhere quiet so we could talk. I did not want to use the word 'private' because I didn't want to alarm him, nor alert him in anyway to the nature of the reason for my call. He said it wouldn't be possible to meet at this office because it was a secure location that was not open to the public, but he would call again on Tuesday night and we would arrange for a time and place to meet. He did not call on that Tuesday so on Wednesday morning I sent another email asking if we could meet after his work.

In less than ten minutes he phoned me back, and we agreed to meet that day at a fast food restaurant in an area. The meeting was scheduled for two o'clock and being early, I got to the restaurant before him. I think in part because of my nervousness I ended up changing where I was sitting three times. Every time I thought I'd found a place that seemed to offer a little privacy, the seats around me would become occupied. If anyone had been watching, they surely would have wondered, what is that woman doing?

It was a humorous thought that made me chuckle, at least for a second. It was in sharp contrast to what I was predominantly feeling considering what I was about to confront this man with. I think I needed a little comic relief to calm myself down. He saw me right away as he entered the restaurant. He apologized for being a little late and asked if I minded him grabbing a drink, offering to get me something as well. I declined, I was already sipping on a coffee. Just a few more minutes and I could begin the conversation I had been anxiously anticipating for the past couple of weeks.

I knew how I wanted to begin but first, we exchanged greetings and asked the standard 'how's life' question. He didn't elaborate but did say that his could be better, that some not so good things had been happening. I thanked him for meeting with me, and said that I too was also going to be the bearer of some not so good news. I just needed to get to the point. I asked if he had any idea why I wanted to talk with him to which he initially said no, he did not. I then added, 'before I do tell you why I wanted to meet with you, you should know that if I had wanted this to go further than between us, I would have filed a complaint three years ago."

He nodded.

I then told him that there had been a sexually explicit message left on my voice mail. I explained how I arrived at the conclusion that it was him, decided at first to let it go but subsequently, through events of the last few months had a change of heart. I needed to be able to speak directly with him if I was going to get any accountability or sense that I had done all that I needed to do in this circumstance. He responded in several different ways.

First, he denied that he was the person that had phoned me, he would never make a call like that. He further said that he actually did have a thought about why I might be wanting to speak with him, based on an encounter I had with him a couple of years before, maybe around the time of the call. He remembered being in a social situation with me where he'd had too much to drink and thought that perhaps he had behaved inappropriately, only in that he'd been rambling on about his personal life, saying things he perhaps should not have.

His thoughts about that were, because he was an officer, and I was an employee, even though I didn't work directly under his supervision, his drunken behaviour would not have been appropriate. In his mind it could have warranted a 'code of conduct' complaint which he says would have been justified and one he would have manned up to. I assured him that he did nothing in that instance that would have been reportable. In my view, we are both adults and nothing inappropriate happened so he can put his mind to rest in that regard.

He said that it was this attitude from me that he remembered, that my responses to him were always kind, and he respected me for that. He said this is also the reason that he returned my call, otherwise he would not have agreed to meet me. He reiterated, he is not the kind of person who would do something like this. He might not always be the nicest guy, and he could be accused of many things, but not for making the kind of call that I was talking about.

What I told him next was not a part of what I had planned to say. I had said in previous chapters that even though I didn't feel I was afraid of confronting him, I would not disclose that I had any physical evidence because he might perceive it to be a threatening gesture and put my safety at risk. At the time I wrote those words, I absolutely felt that way. In this moment, I had no fear and think in hindsight it was my fear that was talking then.

I now told him that before I had come to the conclusion that I might know the person who left the message on my voice mail, I had recorded it and taken the tape to a member who worked in the threat assessment unit. At this point he looked surprised and asked, was it threatening? I replied, no, but it was disturbing and I wanted their feedback. I also wanted him to know that I had them listen to it, to which he followed with, 'well I don't know what was said and I don't want to know'.

Again, another apology from him saying he was sorry that he could not admit to something he didn't do, or else he would. He said he also felt bad because, not only does this not give me closure but also, he didn't like the idea that I had believed it was him for all of this time. His words seemed very sincere, and in fact I must say, forgetting my own reasons for why I was there with this man, I felt a very vulnerable human being sitting only a couple of feet across the table from me. I wish I could say I also felt his innocence, but I did not.

I think he knew as well that I didn't believe him. I could tell by the way he looked at me when my response to his denials was that I wouldn't have come if I wasn't certain that it was him. "People do sound alike," was his response. In fact he said that I sounded like someone else he knew as well. I had to agree, this could be true, and having worked in the world of wiretaps, I know that voice comparison alone is not proof of identification. As a seasoned police officer, he would know this too.

But we were now going around in circles. I was still not buying what he was saying, and I'm sure he could see it in my eyes. The conversation remained amicable, ending with me telling him that he did not have to be concerned with me blind siding him with anything further. I was only concerned now with sorting out the myriad of feelings that I was experiencing in the wake of this meeting. We walked to our respective vehicles which happened to be parked next to each other, exchanged what can only be described as mutual shrugs of resignation, and went on our separate ways.

In the following days, I came to some of the following conclusions. As far as his innocence, all I know is this. If I had been accused by someone of leaving an abusive or threatening message on their phone, the first thing that I would want to do is listen to it. That would be the natural response of an innocent person, if you had nothing to hide. Just ask yourself the same question and see if you agree.

As far as his response affecting my sense of closure, I only need to say this. My challenge was having the courage to confront him because I truly believed that it was him who called me that night. The question of being right about whether it was him or not, was never the motivating issue, it was holding him accountable for what I believed he did do, and giving him the opportunity to respond. I was only seeking for what was true, whatever that would be. And if by some chance he is innocent, then he truly has nothing further to think or worry about. If he is lying, perhaps out of a state of denial, it is now his concern to deal with.

I have been asked how I feel since speaking with him. I know for myself that I feel free, and surprisingly, it's not only with regard to this specific incident, it feels more powerful than that. It's as if my having the courage to speak my truth to this man now, somehow magically righted all the other times in my life that I did not. Was that me forgiving myself? I don't know, all I know is that it was an empowering and totally unforeseen gift to receive, and for that bit of magic, I am totally grateful.

With regard to some other 'unfinished business' that became a part of my story, I am also grateful to have received an update from my friend Scott. He had been waiting to see his step father go to trial for sexually abusing him as a child.

Scott phoned me from the court house. He had just witnessed his step-father get taken away in handcuffs, after being sentenced to seven years in prison for his crimes of abuse.

I am so proud of my friend, for having the willingness and the courage to come forward as he did.

I Took It As A Sign

We all come into life with individual lessons to learn that challenge us to overcome adversity but in the bigger scheme of things, can it all work together for our higher good? Can we really move beyond the negatives in life so we can focus on our potential more than our survival? Before writing this story, my head would have said, 'I think so,' but now in speaking from my heart I would say 'I know so'. We must embrace all of those experiences in life that take away from 'our' knowing ourselves as worthy and wholly lovable human beings and then be brave and dare to look for all that is within, using unconditional love to soften the view of ourselves and others.

And what role does forgiveness play in this transformation? I think it's an absolutely essential part of healing, whether it's forgiveness of self, or forgiveness of others. And while I feel it's one of the most difficult states to achieve, I feel it's the ultimate key in our ability to return to the essence of who we are. It's a letting go of anger and resentment, which too can be one of the harshest and heaviest influences that a body and mind can carry around. And to rid ourselves of these emotional chains can free us to once again be guided by what is in our hearts, and not by what took us from our innate and natural lightness of being.

Another conversation with my friend Sheila comes to mind while we were speaking of her on again, off again communications with her family. She has shared with me situations where she has felt insulted and hurt by their actions and swears that she will never talk to them again. The next thing I know they are back communicating, and she embraces them like nothing has happened. I commented on her ability to forgive, how she takes them back into her life and her heart. She laughingly said, ' I know, sometimes I forgive all the way to forgetting'.

This struck me as a profound way of describing what can potentially happen in all of our lives, and I do think that such a state of mind is possible. As far as how long it takes to get the truths of what can free us, just remember, love waits on welcome, not on time, so you have to wait for nothing but your own willingness to receive. New awareness and healing for me has happened primarily through the acceptance of experiences and feelings previously denied, brought to my attention now through influences greater and well beyond anything I know in this world, which pushed me to write this story.

I know I've touched upon many aspects of life and many areas that deserve further discussion and exploration. And yet despite all the directions I've gone in, from speaking of my own fallout of emotion from sexual abuse to emotional fallout in general, one simple truth keeps emerging: Real change can and does happen when we are willing to look within ourselves. And in the pursuit of knowing and understanding who we are, we'll be assisted in finding the answers to whatever we need in life.

Change has truly become the constant while I've been in the process of this writing, from work to relationships, beginnings and endings, with many ups and downs in between. The only thing that is the same is where I live, down in this little beachfront town and for that I am grateful. I can only hope that if I get the nudge to change that too, it will be aligned with the following card I just picked from my deck of 'Healing with the Fairies' cards.

Before pulling a card I asked to be given one that would be a closing note. I shuffled the deck and the first card I picked was titled, 'Problem Resolved.' I have to say, it did make me chuckle, it couldn't be for me a more appropriate note to end on. May it all come true!

"You're on the cusp of experiencing welcome relief from a problem that's been bothering you. You will have reason to smile, as heaven is working on a solution that is so creative that you'll chuckle with delight at God's sense of humor. Basically, it's a win-win for everyone.

Please don't strain to figure out 'how' this solution will be achieved, or in what form it will manifest. Instead, let yourself enjoy the feelings of excitement and gratitude as you allow heaven to help you.

We only need to keep asking the questions and listening to what gets presented to help guide us in the right direction. Whether it's through a nudge, a dream that repeats itself, a message that keeps showing up, or a hit on the head with a hammer, pay attention.

You never know what or where that 'influence' in life will lead you.

Take it as a sign!

Susan Ashton-Burghley was born in England, and raised in Vancouver B.C. after immigrating with her parents at age three. She has an extensive background in the law enforcement field, working in various capacities, including being a former member of the RCMP and subsequent contract employee. On a personal level, her interests lie in self development and psychology, with a leaning toward a holistic approach which embraces the mind, body and spirit connection with regard to overall health. She has been exposed to those whose behaviour reflects the darkest side of life, not only through her role in law enforcement but also in her personal life, having been the victim of child abuse. Yet despite the disturbing nature of these events, and the ensuing emotional fallout, she has maintained a perspective that is open, optimistic and embracing of life. Her non-fiction story, *I Took It As A Sign*, reflects this, as it is a very candid and personal description of her journey through the emotional mine-field that we all, albeit with trepidation, have to step through. Her account, in its heartfelt intent to only pursue what can improve our lives, helps us to take those first steps needed to clear that field of all that can hurt us, to leaving only that which can help us grow.

D & A
PRESS

.